"I agree wholeheartedly with Justin Earley's priority of living a God-drenched rule of life. It's truly like a healthy jasmine plant growing up on a trellis of good habits that form and shape us into the image of Christ. The earlier we learn this in life, the better off we will be. In your hands is a counterintuitive vision for today's youth who wish to emit a Christlike fragrance to the world around them."

Stephen A. Macchia, founder and president of Leadership Transformations Inc. and author of *Crafting a Rule of Life*

"Justin Whitmel Earley provides a practical pathway to engage with spiritual disciplines that both meets readers where they are and stretches them. Young people who say yes to his invitation will grow in health grounded in deep relationship with God and others."

Tanita Tualla Maddox, national director of generational impact for Young Life and author of *What Gen Z Really Wants to Know About God*

"So many unhelpful forces are shaping the hearts, minds, and lives of our young women and men. What a gift to have the wisdom of *The Common Rule Youth Edition* as a guide to help them cooperate with how God is longing to lead them into the vibrant life of his kingdom!"

Alan Fadling, author of *A Year of Slowing Down*

"As the saying goes, 'Habits eat willpower for breakfast.' In *The Common Rule Youth Edition*, Justin Whitmel Earley helps young readers by providing a practical and inspiring framework for navigating a noisy and distracting world. This resource will speak directly to the hearts of young people and give them fundamental tools for productive habit formation in life and faith."

Brook Mosser, president of Intentional Parents International and host of *The Intentional Parents Podcast*

I0605641

PRAISE FOR *THE COMMON RULE*

"Creation is full of holy rhythms of life. There is a way to live that honors and embodies these rhythms. *The Common Rule* is a beautiful, inviting resource that helps us do just that. It is an important guide to living more deeply rooted in God's life-giving kingdom."

Alan Fadling, president and founder, Unhurried Living

"One of the biggest problems among believers today is their lack of discipline. Consequently, they do not live up to the expectations of Jesus as we can see in the decreasing morality in our country. *The Common Rule* presents a common-sense discipline that any follower of Jesus could use to become a joyful missionary disciple."

Michael Timmis, former chairman of Prison Fellowship Ministries, member of the board of Alpha International and The New Canaan Society

"Habitually choosing what is best over and above what is loud and urgent has never been more difficult than in a culture of perpetual distraction. 'But where do I begin?' people ask. In this book, Justin Earley offers the answer. Follow his lead, and you will find much of your life handed back to you."

John Stonestreet, president of The Chuck Colson Center for Christian Worldview

"It is encouraging to see a new generation of Christians wrestling with the formative power of habits and rituals. Our patterns of life shape our attitudes and actions more than we may realize. *The Common Rule* urges us to consider our habits in a new light and to embrace a new way of life in which we self-consciously limit ourselves in order to pursue what is best for us and for our neighbors."

Trevin Wax, director for Bibles and reference at LifeWay Christian Resources, author of *This Is Our Time: Everyday Myths in Light of the Gospel*

"Although I'm a church leader who has known the Lord for decades, I struggle to find space in my days to actually *abide* in Christ. Instead, I'm tethered to the demands that barrage me through my smartphone. *The Common Rule* offers a practical way back—not only for individuals but also for churches and small groups."

Karen Heetderks Strong, senior director, The Falls Church Anglican, Falls Church, Virginia

"*The Common Rule* is an engaging, relevant, and transforming guide for cultivating spiritual discipline amid the distractions and attractions of life and the daily pressures and challenges of just getting by. The spiritual practices Justin offers are not simply habits and forms adapted for modern life but are habits and forms developed in the painful crucible of personal experience. This book is worth reading and its ways worth pursuing."

Ron Nikkel, president emeritus, Prison Fellowship International

"Books are not meant to be just read. The good ones move you. The great ones change you. I'm now a fan of Justin Whitmel Earley. He's done something that is not so common: he teaches us eight habits that not only change our own lives but more importantly change the lives of those who choose to follow us."

Tommy Spaulding, author of *The Heart-Led Leader* and *It's Not Just Who You Know*

"Justin Earley offers a lifeline to every busy, smartphone addicted, distracted person on earth. In his deeply personal and immensely practical book, he inspires us to find a rhythm that will support our most life-giving relationship of all—our friendship with Jesus."

Ken Shigematsu, pastor of Tenth Church, Vancouver, BC, author of *Survival Guide for the Soul*

"In the spirit of Richard Foster, Eugene Peterson, and so many other reflective authors, this book on the common rule is an exciting contribution to the family God. Each of us needs and longs for a path to deepen our sense of being in this world. So many Christian writers just give us one more self-help book. *The Common Rule* breaks that mold and serves as a call to deeper intimacy with God."

Gary Bradley, The Navigators

"Justin Whitmel Earley's honest walk through anxiety gives hope to anyone who needs a new way. *The Common Rule* becomes an accessible way to move forward in your walk with Christ, whether battling anxiety or simply wanting to find Christ at the center of your life. Earley's fresh look at a liturgical life comes off the page and into your daily life. This book is a refreshing reminder that community, shared meals, fasting, praying, silence, and rest all have deep effects on our lives. In a society of fast food and split families, the return to the table is more important than ever. Earley lived the fast-paced world of no margin where everyone has free access to his life, yet in the pages of this book, we see he has found another way–another way for us all."

Diana M. Shiflett, pastor of spiritual formation, Naperville Covenant Church, author of *Spiritual Practices in Community*

"When someone asks how you're doing and you always find yourself answering, 'So busy and crazy,' it might be time for a change. *The Common Rule* offers practical wisdom on how to slowly but deliberately restructure our lives, and it shows us that when we embrace limitations, we paradoxically gain the freedom we long for."

John Dyer, author of *From the Garden to the City: The Redeeming and Corrupting Power of Technology*

"I'm thankful for the Common Rule because it is a practical tool to save me from the tyranny of machine-like productivity. The book and practices remind me that I am a human being and not a human doing. Read this book and save yourself from the tyranny!"

David M. Bailey, executive director of Arrabon, coauthor of *Race, Class, and the Kingdom of God*

"In the present age, we are settling to be informed when the call is to be transformed. I'm no Luddite, but we must rethink the way technology and busyness are affecting our loves. *The Common Rule* not only has incredible practical advice for daily and weekly rhythms, it also opens our eyes to see the water we're swimming in. Every church should consider using this as a resource for formation."

AJ Sherrill, author of *Enneagram and the Way of Jesus*, lead pastor at Mars Hill Bible Church, Grand Rapids, Michigan

"I love the practicality of this book. Justin Whitmel Earley understands and embodies the reality that we show what we love and value by the daily habits of our lives."

Mark Scandrette, author of *Free and Practicing the Way of Jesus*, and coauthor of *Belonging and Becoming*

JUSTIN WHITMEL EARLEY
with JESSE FLOREA

THE COMMON RULE *Youth Edition*

GROWING YOUR FAITH IN A DISTRACTED WORLD

YOUNG READERS EDITION

An imprint of InterVarsity Press
Downers Grove, Illinois

InterVarsity Press
P.O. Box 1400 | Downers Grove, IL 60515-1426
ivpress.com | email@ivpress.com

InterVarsity Press® is the publishing division of InterVarsity Christian Fellowship/USA®. For more information, visit intervarsity.org.

Cover design: Faceout Studio, Addie Lutzo
Interior design: Daniel van Loon
Cover image: © Diane Labombarbe / DigitalVision Vectors via Getty Image

ISBN 978-1-5140-1043-3 (print) | ISBN 978-1-5140-1044-0 (digital)

Printed in the United States of America ♾

Library of Congress Cataloging-in-Publication Data
A catalog record for this book is available from the Library of Congress.

30 29 28 27 26 25 | 13 12 11 10 9 8 7 6 5 4 3 2 1

TO ALL MY NIECES AND NEPHEWS,

with great hope that each of you

would fall in love with following Jesus.

CONTENTS

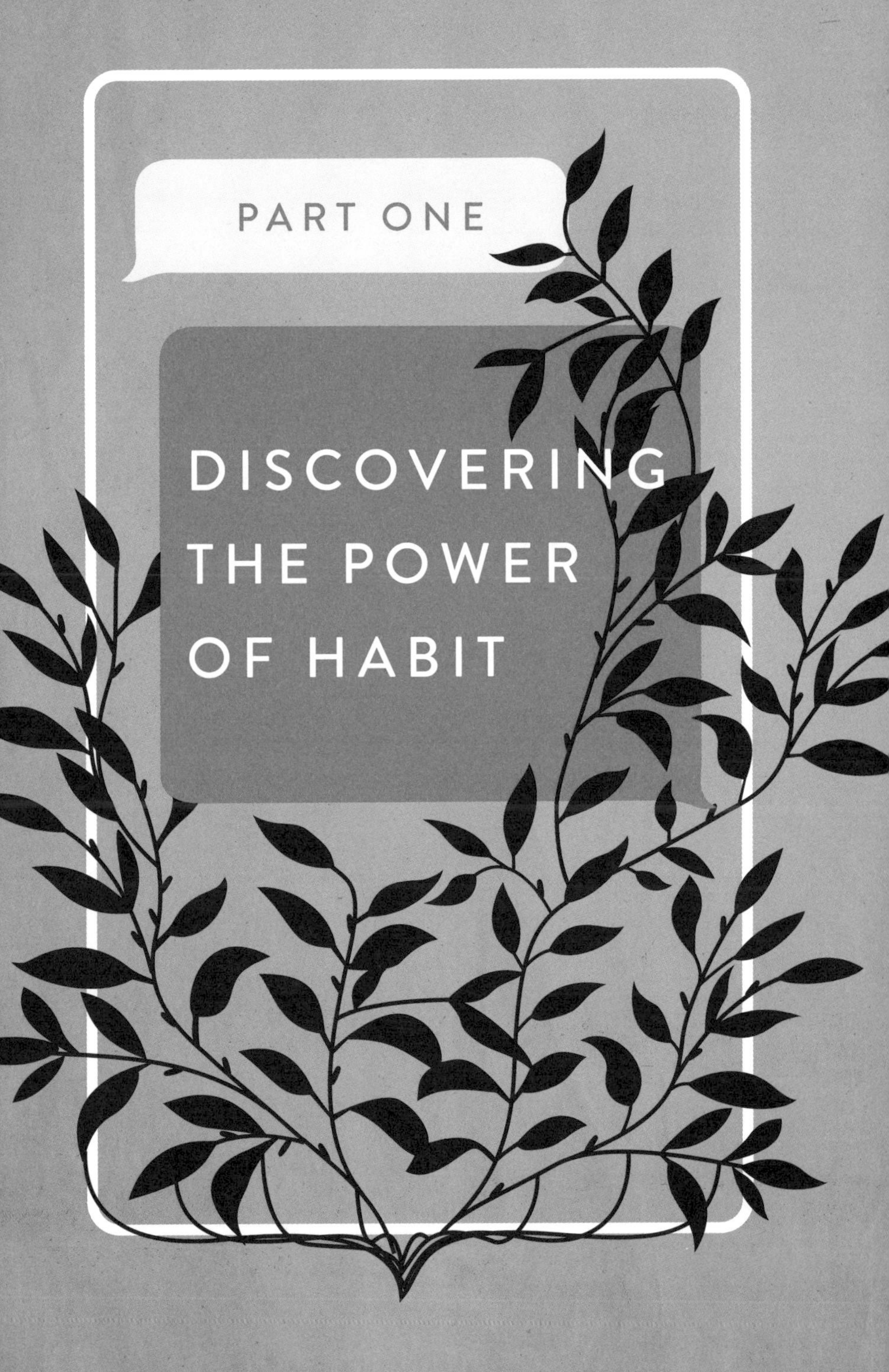

PART ONE

DISCOVERING THE POWER OF HABIT

WHEN HABITS GO WRONG

It was midnight on an ordinary Saturday night when I woke in a dreadful panic. Sweating and shaking, I sat up in bed. The feeling was so intense I expected to find something terrible had happened. But all was quiet.

I woke up my wife and tried to explain what I was feeling. It was like my heart had rung the alarm bells for no reason. Finally, after calming down, I fell back asleep.

The next night, the same thing happened. Only this time, I couldn't fall back asleep. The next day, I was a zombie. Fear worked through me like a virus. I dreaded the moment that night when I would have to lie back down with my panicked thoughts.

Sure enough, that night it happened again. Which is why I ended up in the emergency room at three in the morning. The doctor told me nothing was wrong, that I was just showing symptoms of clinical anxiety and panic attacks. He assured me—as if it were comforting—that this was *very common*. So he gave me a bottle of sleeping pills and told me I needed to slow down.

Of course, I had no idea how to slow down.

EVERYTHING IS FINE

As far as I knew, I wasn't stressed or worried about anything. Everything was fine! After graduating from college, I married my wonderful wife and we moved to China where we served as missionaries for a few years. We would have stayed even longer, except that something very unusual happened.

One day, while out on a walk, in the space of ten minutes I came across a drug dealer, a prostitute, a thief, and a government protestor.

Guess which action stood out the most?

Openly selling drugs on the street. Nope.

Prostitution. Uh-uh.

Getting rid of stolen electronics at bargain prices. Guess again.

All three of these activities were normal in China. I'd seen them hundreds of times, and they were viewed as legitimate ways to make money.

But in the years we'd lived in China, I'd *never* seen a political protest. The consequences for opposing the government are way too high. Yet there she was. I watched as a young woman unfurled a sign that said, "The judicial system in China is broken, the people in the countryside are being oppressed—" I never got to read the rest of the sign because the woman was quickly arrested and taken away.

As I continued my walk, I reflected on the four activities I'd just witnessed. Three would've been considered against the law in many countries. And only one was a brave act of love for a neighbor. Yet the young woman who stood up for oppressed people was the only one punished. And that didn't sit well with me.

That was the day I realized the power that law and business have to shape the world. And that was also the day I felt the Lord telling me that if I wanted to follow him, I should do it in those arenas. That's where God wanted me to be a missionary, not in China.

I listened to God's call. My wife, Lauren, and I moved to Washington, DC, where I went to Georgetown Law and graduated at the top of my class. Soon we had two sons, and I landed a job as a mergers and acquisitions attorney at the best big law firm in Richmond, Virginia. My family and best friends lived in Richmond, so we moved down there to live happily ever after—or so I thought.

Life was going great.

Well, one thing wasn't great. I was tired. Really tired. In the years after finishing my undergraduate degree at the University of Virginia, I had tackled life with a voracious intensity. I wanted to be good at everything I did. In China, I'd wake up early to study Mandarin and stay up late to hang out with fellow missionaries and Chinese friends.

In law school, my life became an endless series of calendar alerts, appointments, résumé-building activities, and studying late into the night. But every student at Georgetown was like that. Being overwhelmed by ambition was a way of life in law school, so I went along with it. I thought that was how you got to be a top law student, land a big job, and become a successful lawyer—by saying *yes* to everything and *no* to nothing.

I was too busy, totally overcommitted, and trying to keep up with a chaotic schedule. But I thought I could handle it because I had a calling.

Looking back, I can see how my calling turned into calamity. I intended to tackle injustice and change the world for Jesus. Instead I was the one being changed. My habits looked like everyone else's.

Still, this life was working for me . . . until it wasn't.

THE MISSIONARY GETS CONVERTED

After my late-night trip to the emergency room, I started taking sleeping pills, which began the darkest phase I have ever known. The pills blacked me out for a couple of hours every night, but I soon discovered they came with horrible side effects. Enormous mood swings during the day, hallucinogenic nightmares, even suicidal thoughts—those were all happening to me.

MY HEAD SAID ONE THING—THAT GOD LOVES ME NO MATTER WHAT I DO. BUT MY HABITS SAID ANOTHER—THAT I NEED TO KEEP STRIVING AND ACHIEVING IN ORDER TO REMAIN LOVED.

This led to a long stretch of time when I needed either pills or alcohol to fall asleep. Eventually I ditched the sleeping pills—thank God—but the drinking remained. And so did a stubborn question: *How does a missionary end up being the one who needs saving?*

Answering this question wasn't easy. I worshiped busyness, accolades, and success. My habits and routines had trained my body to deal with anxiety and keep going. All the years of a nonstop schedule to earn my place in the world had finally rubbed off on my heart.

My head said one thing—that God loves me no matter what I do. But my habits said another—that I need to keep striving and achieving in order to remain loved.

In the end, my habits wore down my mind, broke down my body, and ate away at my soul. That's why what happened during the next year of my life was so important.

THINK ABOUT IT . . .

1. Think of an experience—even something you heard, saw, or read—that changed your thinking. What was the experience, and how did your thinking change?

2. After reading about the habits the author developed, do you notice something about your own habits that you hadn't noticed before? What is it you notice?

3. Rate your busyness on a scale from 1 to 10:

1 — 2 — 3 — 4 — 5 — 6 — 7 — 8 — 9 — 10

Just chillin' | Just right | Just tryin' to hang on

4. This chapter suggests that when your habits (behaviors) go one way but your head (thoughts) goes another, your habits usually win. Like deciding to get up early every day, but having the habit of hitting snooze on your alarm. Have you experienced a time like that?

WHAT IS A HABIT?

When I was young, my mom planted Carolina jasmine in the garden next to our brick garage. Jasmine is beautiful, but it is also a twining vine plant. If not directed, its prolific shoots spread toward other plants, overtaking and eventually killing them.

My mom also built a trellis next to the brick wall. The wooden framework directed the jasmine up and away from the other plants. After a few seasons, yellow blossoms covered the whole wall.

I still remember how that brick turned from something barren to something beautiful. And I still remember the way the fragrance filled the backyard with the thick smell of spring.

Our lives are like a jasmine plant growing on a trellis of habits.

At best, we're made to grow upward, blossom beautifully, and fill the earth with the rich fragrance of God's love and truth. The Bible puts it this way: "Our lives are a Christ-like fragrance rising up to God" (2 Corinthians 2:15).

At worst, we grow into a twisted jumble. We shoot off sideways in ways we weren't meant to, often snarling into something that hurts us and destroys those around us.

Without a thoughtful framework to guide our growth, we're likely to form habits that are destructive. Building a trellis of healthy habits is a way to acknowledge the good ways God designed us, and the good limits he offers us.

A *habit* is a behavior that occurs automatically, over and over, and often unconsciously. The fact is, we all live according to habits that shape our lives. But we don't often think much about them. A study from Duke University suggests that as much as 40 percent of the actions we take every day are not the products of choices but of habits.[1]

Take your daily schedule or your posting on social media. Think about your internet history or how you spent your mornings last weekend. Look at the time you spend with family versus the time you spend looking at a screen during a normal day.

These things define vast portions of our lives. While we would like to think we've carefully chosen these actions, most often we haven't even given them a second thought.

This wouldn't be so bad if it weren't for the fact that habits form much more than our schedules—they form our hearts.

In the months after my anxiety crash-landed me in the ER, my wife and I had sketched out a program of habits to get my heart to believe the peace that my head knew but my body refused. I didn't think any of the habits we'd scribbled down were life-changing. There were daily habits of prayer and taking time away from my phone. Weekly habits included a day of rest and talking more with friends. Nothing mind-blowing.

So my heart was still a twisted mess when I met up with Matt and Steve, my two best friends, at a restaurant to talk to them about these habits. It was a night of good conversation about living with better daily and weekly rhythms. And my friends were going to keep me accountable.

A *HABIT* IS A BEHAVIOR THAT OCCURS AUTOMATICALLY, OVER AND OVER, AND OFTEN UNCONSCIOUSLY.

At the time, I hadn't heard of a *keystone habit*—a micro shift that brings about macro effects. I didn't think a few good habit shifts would change my life. But to my surprise, they did.

THE SCIENCE OF HABIT

In the book *The Power of Habit*, it says, "When a habit is formed, the brain stops fully participating in decision-making. The patterns we have unfold automatically."[2]

In other words, whether we are aware of it or not, we all have habits that shape how we live our lives. And that can be a good thing, because when we act on our habits, it frees up brain space for other thoughts. That's why we can walk between classes and suddenly arrive in our next class without thinking about a single step we've taken. Instead of consciously deciding where to go, we've been talking with a friend or thinking about tonight's game.

Scientifically, habits help our brains to be multi-functional. This is really useful in general, but it has downsides.

And if we're acting out a bad habit—one that reinforces an addiction, perpetuates a harmful pattern of thought, or encourages mindless submission to technology—we don't have much power to fight back.

Think about your phone. How often do you check it? Research shows the average teen looks at it more than 100 times a day, for over five hours on average. Some check it nearly 500 times a day![3] (Even adults average over three hours a day.) Students use their phone at school and at home. All day. Every day.

There's something unhealthy and maybe even wrong about that. We can tell ourselves over and over that we want to break free from that tiny screen and experience more of real life. But the part of our brain that changes a habit is exactly the part that gets shut out when the autopilot of habit turns on.

When we're on autopilot, our choices—even the unconscious ones—shape us and form us, and we develop patterns that we would never consciously choose.

THE THEOLOGY OF HABIT

This is why to fully understand habits we must think of habits as liturgies. A *liturgy* is a pattern of words or actions repeated regularly as a way of worship. I'm not only talking about what we sing or say at church; we worship anything by honoring and being devoted. Worship through liturgy involves our thoughts and our time and our lives. For example, I say the Lord's Prayer every night because I want the words of Jesus' prayer to sink down into my bones.

So do you see how similar liturgy is to habit? They're both something repeated over and over that influences who we are. The only difference is that a liturgy admits that it's an act of worship. Our habits often obscure what we're really worshiping, but that doesn't mean we're not worshiping something. Because worship is often a reflection of our time and attention. And our habits reveal what we each believe is most worthy of our time and attention.

A *LITURGY* IS A PATTERN OF WORDS OR ACTIONS REPEATED REGULARLY AS A WAY OF WORSHIP.

So the question for us is: *What are we worshiping?*

When we combine the idea that our habits are liturgies of worship, along with the scientific insight that our brains aren't totally engaged when our habits are playing out, it explains how our unconscious habits form much more than our schedules—they form our hearts.

Take a look at the chart on the next page to see how this works in a daily routine.

All of these liturgies of wrong belief play a part in creating anxiety. And anxiety is a growing problem. Studies show that one out of three teenagers will experience an anxiety disorder. Between the pressure to succeed that many feel from parents and teachers, a world that often feels scary and out of control, and the demands of social media, it's hard not to feel anxious sometimes.[4]

But go back and look at the chart. Which one do you think is especially dangerous? It's the last one: the freedom liturgy.

We assume the good life comes from having the freedom to do whatever we want in each moment. But when we live out the "no-limits-none-ever" freedom liturgy, we actually miss out on the good life.

What if the good life comes not from having the ability to do what we want, but from having the ability to do what we

HABIT	LITURGY OF WRONG BELIEF
Wake up exhausted again, because I never get to bed on time.	My body will be fine. I can push harder than regular people. I am a god.
Check my texts and social media on my phone before getting out of bed.	I can miss a quiet time, but I can't miss what's happening. Unless I'm posting and getting followed, I'm not worth anything.
Grab fast food or dinner in my room, while everyone else in my family eats together.	Being too busy is normal. To be important, I need to stay busy.
Keep my phone on and within arm's reach at all times.	The most important thing is the most recent thing. The best way to love my neighbors is to stay updated on friends, school drama, and new memes, not to do focused work.
Even when the best word to describe life is "scattered" or "busy," resist any rules that restrict technology use and extracurricular activities.	To limit myself is to restrict my freedom. The good life comes from choosing to do what I want, when I want.

were made for? What if true freedom comes from choosing the right limits, not avoiding all limits?

As I look back on that night in the restaurant with my friends, it was a defining moment in my life, because I finally surrendered the keystone habit of freedom. I decided that following a framework of limits was a better way of life.

WHAT IF TRUE FREEDOM COMES FROM CHOOSING THE RIGHT LIMITS, NOT AVOIDING ALL LIMITS?

And that's when everything changed.

I had lived my whole life thinking that all limits ruin freedom—when all along it's the opposite: the right limits *create* freedom.

This wasn't an overnight realization. As my life began to change, I began to wonder why surrendering the freedom liturgy and accepting limitations was so hard for me. I began to wonder how I had come to believe such a bizarre definition of success and freedom. And I wondered if there were living examples of a better freedom.

I found the answer in the life of Jesus.

THINK ABOUT IT . . .

1. How have you seen your life grow out of control or in dangerous directions? How can a framework actually provide freedom and a pathway to personal success?

2. Look at the liturgy of wrong belief chart. The author describes these as liturgies of worship to performance, rush, hurry, and anxiety. Describe what *liturgy* means in your own words based on the chart.

3. How can small, ordinary habits have big spiritual effects?

4. The author asks, “What if the good life comes not from having the ability to do what we want, but from having the ability to do what we were made for? What if true freedom comes from choosing the right limits, not avoiding all limits?” Do you agree? How can our pursuit of freedom trap us in dangerous patterns?

JESUS AS THE GOOD MASTER

No one surrendered more freedom than Jesus. The Bible tells us that Jesus "gave up his divine privileges" and "he humbled himself" (Philippians 2:7-8). Jesus went from God's all-powerful son to a helpless infant. He went from speaking the universe into existence by his Word, to not being able to speak a word.

But it didn't stop there. He did not just become human. He became a poor human who grew into a homeless human. A human who loved with such power that he became a threat to those in power, so they tortured and killed him. Jesus submitted to the ultimate limitation: to be snuffed out of the world in death. But why? Why would he do this?

For love.

For the love he has for you and me.

In his letter to the Philippians, the apostle Paul wrote that because Jesus was willing to submit to the limitation of death, he was exalted (see Philippians 2:6-11). When Jesus rose from the dead and walked out of the grave, he danced on death itself. Because of Jesus' sacrifice, anyone who chooses to surrender their life and believe in him will also rise with him.

The key thing to notice here is how Jesus' actions are the exact opposite of what the first humans did in the Garden of Eden. There, Adam and Eve rejected God's authority and ate the forbidden fruit. And their rejections of limitations brought the ultimate limitations of sin and death into the world.

Jesus shows us a better way. But his way might not seem logical, because his way says the way down is the way up. The way to victory is through surrender. The way to freedom is through limitation.

JESUS SHOWS US A BETTER WAY—THAT THE WAY DOWN IS THE WAY UP.

As I developed habits that often looked opposite of those around me, it changed my personal and work life. By putting limits on my work schedule and technology use, I became better at my job. One of my habits is to turn off my phone for one hour each evening. Surprisingly, I found most of my clients and colleagues were fine getting a call back an hour later when I turned my phone back on.

My life was becoming more focused, and I saw positive effects in my mental and spiritual health. So I started talking about habits—a lot! I probably annoyed many of my friends, who had to hear about it over and over.

One day when I was explaining some of my new habits to my pastor, he responded, "Oh, I see. You've crafted your own rule of life."

"What's a rule of life?" I asked.

He explained that a "rule of life" is a term used to describe a pattern of habits that form who we are. In fact, the word *rule* comes from the Latin word *regula*, a word associated with a bar or trellis on which a plant grows. (Hmmm . . . sound familiar?)

Fittingly, the best way to understand a rule of life or a program of habits is by picturing a trellis. We are always growing and changing, but when there is no framework to guide us in a healthy direction, we turn into a twisted vine of decay. Vines that decay can't produce good fruit or flowers, just like it's hard for us to produce a fruitful life when we're growing in unhealthy directions.

But when we attach our life to a trellis of keystone habits centered around Jesus, we can grow in a healthy direction (see Galatians 5:22-23). Simply put, a rule of life is intended to guide our life in the direction of purpose and love instead of toward chaos and decay.

GOD'S RULE OF LIFE

If we want to be attentive to who we are becoming, we must begin with a framework of habits.

For example, it's important to learn the right theological truths about God, but it's equally necessary to put that theology into practice. If we say we believe truth but refuse to practice truth, we become hypocrites. I happen to think the Jesus way is pretty compelling, and that it's tough to know Jesus and not want to follow him. Even so, I've known a lot of people who have

> A RULE OF LIFE IS INTENDED TO GUIDE OUR LIFE IN THE DIRECTION OF PURPOSE AND LOVE INSTEAD OF TOWARD CHAOS AND DECAY.

walked that divide of knowing Jesus—or thinking they know him—but not following.

It's only when our habits match our worldview that we become someone who doesn't just know about God, we become someone who actually loves God. But how does that work? *What does it look like to love God?*

Good question! The Bible tells us that "loving God means keeping his commandments, and his commandments are not burdensome" (1 John 5:3).

In case you have an allergy to the word *commandments*, stick with me here. What kind of commandments are we talking about?

I'm glad you asked, because people have been asking that same question for centuries. In fact, a Jewish Pharisee—someone who followed all the commandments and knew them all by heart—asked Jesus which of the commands was the greatest. Jesus said that all the laws and commandments come down to just two things:

- Love the Lord your God with all your heart and with all your soul and with all your mind.
- Love your neighbor as yourself.

To find purpose, peace, fulfillment, and direction in life, the Bible tells us we were made for two things: to love God and to love our neighbor. Now there's a rule of life we can follow!

HEAD, HABITS, AND HEART

After talking with my pastor, I realized that I had stumbled upon some ancient wisdom with my little program of habits. It was a rule of life that I had applied specifically to my deformed modern liturgies of work and technology. But as I talked with my friends and family about how living according to a rule of life was changing my life, many of them suggested I share it so others could try it too.

THE GOAL HERE IS AGREEMENT OF HEAD, HABIT, AND HEART.

I took some of my favorite habits, put them together in a PDF, and called it "The Common Rule," because it was intended as a common practice for common people. Then I emailed it to about fifteen friends.

Within a week, it was forwarded to hundreds of people. From there, it kept going.

Since I began writing about the Common Rule, I've learned there are people of all ages who are like me—absolutely starved for an example of how to meaningfully order daily life in a way that unites their head, habits, and heart.

The more I read and talked to others, the more convinced I was that we have a common problem. By ignoring the ways habits form us, we've adopted a hidden rule of life: the American rule of life. And the American rule of life is a rigorous program of anxiety, depression, consumerism, injustice, and vanity.

Remember: the goal here is agreement of head, habit, and heart. *It's not about doing the practices or getting them right!* It's what we discover—about God, about others, and about ourselves—while we do the practices.

But this isn't just a personal matter. It is a public imperative. Talking about Jesus—while ignoring the way of Jesus—has created an American Christianity that is far more American than it is Christian. We pay attention to the message of Jesus, yet ignore his practices. This has not only led people like me into a devastating life crisis, it has also created a country of Christians whose everyday lives don't reflect their actual faith. How else do we explain Christians who preach a radical gospel of Jesus while following the usual habits of American life?

There is a better way. It is the way of Jesus.

As you continue reading this book, my prayer for you is the same as it was for me:

> *Let us see that habits shape the heart. Let us stop fearing that limits are a threat to our freedom. Let us see that the right limitations are the way to the good life. Let us build a trellis for our lives to grow on. Let us craft a common rule of life, one that unites our heads and our habits, growing us into the lovers of God and neighbor we were created to be.*

Are you ready to have your life changed?

THINK ABOUT IT . . .

1. When you think about all the limits that Jesus accepted out of his love for you, which one stands out the most? Why?

2. Everyone has a rule of life. If you had to describe the rule of life that you live by (it may even be subconscious), what kinds of values and habits would be in it?

3. React to this statement: "People, for their own sake, tried to become limitless and the world was ruined. Jesus, for our sake, became limited and the world was saved."

4. How do you see the American rule of life lived out in your habits? What's one habit you'd like to change?

5. What words would you use to describe "the way of Jesus"?

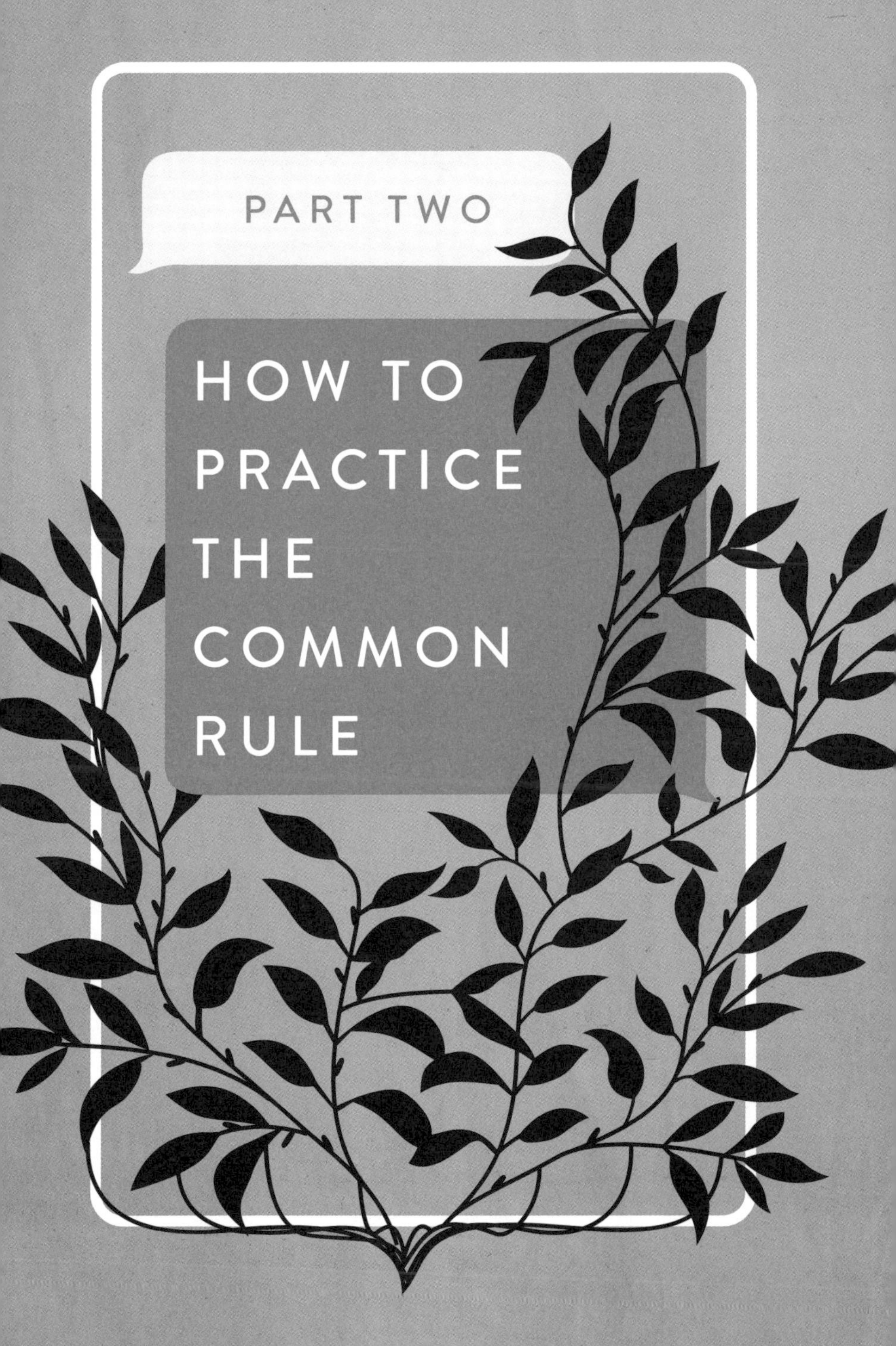
PART TWO
HOW TO PRACTICE THE COMMON RULE

THE EIGHT HABITS OF THE COMMON RULE

In Ohio, there's a rule that you can't make silly faces at a dog. A law in Georgia says you must eat fried chicken with your hands. And a rule in Kentucky forbids walking down the street with an ice cream cone in your back pocket.

None of those rules are part of the Common Rule, although I do agree with the rule in Alabama that makes it illegal to drive a car blindfolded.[1]

For the purpose of this book, a *rule* is defined as a set of habits that you commit to follow in order to grow in your love of God and your neighbor. The Common Rule is made up of eight habits—four daily and four weekly.

THE DAILY HABITS

- kneeling prayer at morning, midday, and bedtime
- one meal with others
- one hour with your phone off
- Scripture before phone in the morning

THE WEEKLY HABITS

- one hour of conversation with a friend
- four hours of physical activity
- fast from something for twenty-four hours
- sabbath rest

Each habit serves a specific purpose and corresponds to different dimensions of life. The four dimensions are *love of God*, *love of neighbor*, *embrace*, and *resistance*.

IF YOU'RE UNABLE TO KNEEL, YOU CAN CHANGE YOUR POSTURE BY TURNING YOUR PALMS UP, RAISING YOUR HEAD TO THE SKY, OR EVEN BREATHING DEEPLY.

Love of God. You were made to love and be loved by God. Only in the light of his love will you see who you really are, feel how you are supposed to feel, and discover what you should do with your days. Therefore, four of the habits of the Common Rule are pointed toward opening our eyes to who God is, accepting the love he freely offers, and returning the gaze that has always been fixed on us.

- sabbath
- fasting
- prayer
- Scripture before phone

Love of neighbor. The word *neighbor* here is used in the New Testament sense of the word. In Jesus' parable of the Good Samaritan (see Luke 10:29-37), he defined a neighbor as anyone and everyone in our lives: family, friends, strangers, and even enemies.

When we think of creating better habits, we often think about how habits can improve *us*. But nothing could be further from the purpose of the Common Rule. These next four habits encourage spending meaningful time with *others*. They force us to interrupt our busy schedules for the sake of community. They encourage us to put down our devices and become more present with one another.

- meals
- conversation
- phone off
- physical activity

Before reading the Common Rule, a friend asked me if the habits helped us care for ourselves. My answer was, "Yes, because we're made to be happy when we're focusing on others." These habits are designed to help us spend our days with others, rather than just by ourselves.

Embrace. Embrace is a reminder of how much good exists in the world God made. God's presence—not his absence—is the primary fact of the world. And the primary truth of being created in God's image is that we need each other. Humans were made for community—not isolation. We're made to love each other—not harm each other. In the habits of embrace, we train our bodies and our hearts to love God as he actually is and to turn to our neighbor as we were made to do.

> A *RULE* IS A SET OF HABITS THAT YOU COMMIT TO FOLLOW IN ORDER TO GROW IN YOUR LOVE OF GOD AND YOUR NEIGHBOR.

- sabbath
- prayer
- meals
- conversation

Resistance. When we practice resistance, we acknowledge that evil and suffering are very real, though they aren't how the world was made to be.

Our world is full of a thousand invisible habits of fear, anger, anxiety, and envy. If we do nothing and float along with society, we unconsciously (and consciously!) adopt the very things that tear us apart.

The Bible warns against this, saying, "Don't copy the behavior and customs of this world, but let God transform you into a new person by changing the way you think. Then you will learn to know God's will for you, which is good and pleasing and perfect" (Romans 12:2).

So to understand God's will and follow his purpose for us, we must take up the fight. We need to open our eyes to the way media form us in fear and hate, the way screens form us in absence from others, and the way excess trains us to love ourselves above all else.

The habits of resistance are:

- fasting
- Scripture before phone
- phone off
- physical activity

THINK ABOUT IT . . .

1. After learning what the four daily and four weekly habits are, which one do you think would make the biggest difference in your life? Why?

2. Do you feel you're better at loving God or loving others? Why did God call us to do both?

3. Rate your excitement level on starting to practice the Common Rule:

1 — 2 — 3 — 4 — 5 — 6 — 7 — 8 — 9 — 10

Meh | It might help | Let's get started already!

DAILY HABITS

1 Kneeling prayer at morning, midday, and and bedtime

2 One meal with others

3 One hour with phone off

4 Scripture before phone

WEEKLY HABITS

1 One hour of conversation with a friend	2 Four hours of physical activity
3 Fast from something for twenty-four hours	4 Sabbath rest

TIME TO PRACTICE THE COMMON RULE

A pair of cows were out talking in a field. One cow said to the other, "Have you heard about the mad cow disease that's going around?"

"Yeah," the other cow said. "That makes me glad I'm a penguin."

Yes, it's a bad joke. But it illustrates an important truth about self-awareness.

Denying a fact doesn't mean it's not a fact. Being a cow makes cows susceptible to mad cow disease, just like being a human makes us susceptible to human "diseases" of envy, busyness, anxiety, and exhaustion.

Learning something new is good, and this book is meant to help you learn to become self-aware. So until you put what you've learned here into action, it doesn't do you any good. In other words, these rules need to be practiced, not simply read.

These habits changed my life for the better physically, mentally, and spiritually. But they didn't just change my life, they changed the lives of the people around me, including my wife, my friends, and many others.

As the name of this book suggests, *The Common Rule* isn't meant for just the individual. It's a common rule that is common to all people, therefore it's ideally practiced with other people. Change—even personal change—almost always happens within a community where people support each other, process what they're learning, and keep each other accountable to goals.

Because of that, I strongly encourage you to invite friends or family members to try out the Common Rule with you.

Here are some ways you can do that.

PRACTICE, PRACTICE, PRACTICE

Studies show it takes at least two to three weeks to create new habits. So before we dig deeper into each of these rules, I want to talk about the best ways to practice them.

For a month. Committing to practice the Common Rule alongside other people for one month is best. By following these habits for four weeks, you can replace the unseen habits you never knew you had. This also gives you the truest experience of the habits and allows the best chance of having these rules stick to your life going forward.

When trying out a month of the Common Rule individually or with a group, you might find it helpful to create a chart for the week or even for the month. Remember, any new pattern of habits seems overwhelming until you realize there's a groove to it. The Common Rule will feel like a lot until you realize the rhythms lighten your load, they don't add to it. This usually takes a few weeks to sink in.

For a week. If you aren't quite ready for a month, try a week.

Eight of the chapters in this book focus specifically on the daily and weekly habits. Read one chapter each day (each will take about ten minutes). You'll finish one week later, on the same day of the week you started.

After you read the chapter, try that habit right away. There's no reason to wait and practice all the habits at once. Just read a chapter a day and experiment with that habit that day.

Below is a template for reading and trying each of the habits in the Common Rule in one week. This plan assumes you will try this in a group. If you don't have a group, I strongly suggest finding at least one other person. It's hard to make new habits alone!

Try one or two. If you'd rather browse the book and try out a habit or two, that's wonderful. There's no reason you can't skip around and read about the habit that interests you most. Many people find experimenting with one keystone habit is the best way to begin trying the Common Rule. This will give you an idea of how changing one habit can lead to positive change in other areas of your life.

Based on comments I've received, kneeling in prayer and Scripture before phone can be the most impactful daily habits to start with. By kneeling in prayer, it helps structure your day and put yourself in a position of humility before an all-powerful God. Reading the Bible before looking at your phone in the morning sounds simple. But this one small change has proven to have a powerful impact.

DAY	READ		HABIT TO TRY
1	DAILY HABITS	1	Try kneeling prayer at least once.
2		2	Intentionally eat a meal with a friend or family member.
3		3	Pick one hour to turn your phone off.
4		4	Before you use your phone today, read Scripture.
5	WEEKLY HABITS	1	Have an intentional one-on-one conversation with someone.
6		2	Estimate the number of hours you've done a physical activity this week. If it's not four, try to exercise with a friend.
7		3	Fast from something today.
8		4	Make today a sabbath or write out some ideas to plan your next sabbath.

As far as weekly habits, try an hour of conversation with a friend and taking a sabbath. At first these can sound like opposites, but both involve slowing down and focusing on friendship—with others and with God.

THE LIGHT BURDEN

One of the biggest (and most understandable) misconceptions people have about the Common Rule is that it will be a lot of work and take a lot of time. Don't worry, it won't. Starting the Common Rule during a stressful season or time of change can be a great idea. In fact, if you're feeling overwhelmed, you're holding the right book!

CREATING NEW HABITS IS HARD. BUT ANYTHING WORTH DOING IS HARD.

At the same time, I acknowledge that creating new habits is hard. But anything worth doing is hard.

So I won't tell you the Common Rule is not hard. What I will tell you is that it is freeing. You'll find once new Common Rule habits are established, they don't take up time and mental space. They work in the background. They're designed to free up your time, create meaningful space for relationships, turn your energy toward good work, and focus your presence on the God who made you and loves you.

That's not constricting. It's liberating. And you were made for it.

THINK ABOUT IT . . .

1. Can you think of family members or friends you'd like to do the Common Rule with? Write down their names, and ask them to join you.

2. What's your plan? Try for a month? A week? One or two habits? Circle one, and then do it!

3. This chapter talks about being self-aware and examining your life. Why is this important? Why do most people fail to do this?

4. Read Matthew 11:28-30. What do Jesus' words mean to you? How do these verses relate to the Common Rule?

PART THREE
DAILY
AND WEEKLY
HABITS

DAILY HABIT 1

KNEELING PRAYER AT MORNING, MIDDAY, AND BEDTIME

> *Your kingdom come, your will be done, on earth as it is in heaven.*
> JESUS (MATTHEW 6:10 ESV)

When people ask me what I do, I often say, "I change things with words."

Here is what I mean. When two companies have a deal they want to make, they turn to a corporate lawyer, like me, to create a contract that takes their concept and makes it a concrete reality. Corporate lawyers move negotiations forward by choosing the most convincing words. We minimize risk by making sure a contract has all the right words. And at the closing of the deal, we create a new reality by actually saying these words: "Ladies and gentlemen, we are closed. Congratulations."

If you think about it, it's amazing. One moment, no merger existed that united two entities, and the next moment something new exists—simply because of words. Words can create new realities. And even small words can have an enormous impact.

As I look back on my career, it sometimes looks strange. I have been some combination of a missionary, a writer, and a lawyer. But when I think about words, it all makes sense: my life has been a life of words. I've been in the business of words, trying to convince the world that there is truth, there is beauty, and there is order.

Understanding the power of small words is central to understanding the significance of daily prayer. We all desire to shape our chaotic days into lives with meaning. That begins with punctuating our days with words: the words of prayer. I believe in the power of words—and especially words of prayer—to shape the world.

A WORLD MADE BY WORDS

The world began with words.

At first, the majestic power of God's voice spoke light into existence. Then came planets, plasmas, penguins, pineapples, and polar ice caps. When God spoke, the universe took shape.

Words brought order to chaos and form to the formless. But the power of words didn't stop with God. Their power passed to us humans—the part of creation that was made in God's image.

One of the most fascinating moments of the whole creation narrative is the moment when God handed the power of words to humans. God spends days moving in and out of a divine rhythm where he speaks the world into existence and then sits back to say, "Good! Very good!"

Then God turns to humans and says, "Your turn"—or more formally, "Be fruitful and multiply." How did he pass on the task to us? By words. How are we to begin this task? Of course, by words. Adam's first job is to come alongside God and name the animals of the world (see Genesis 2:19-20). As the first poet—and zoologist—God invites Adam to work with him to speak order into the world by the power of words.

REFRAMING YOUR DAY

At the beginning of each new day, we begin with words. Just as God ordered the world in love, we can use the words of prayer to order each part of our day in love.

Every day of my life, I have woken with a kind of prayer. Depending on my life stage or how I felt, my prayer has been radically different.

In high school, it was, "Oh why, oh why, does first period start so early?" Or maybe, "Please don't let anyone find out what happened last night."

In college, my prayers became inarticulate groans. Something like, "Oh please let it not matter that I'm missing that class."

More recently, my prayers have been, "I should've gone to bed earlier. Please help me get that project done because I'm tired."

Notice how throughout my life, my day has begun with a profound sense of wishing something was different. Usually it revolves around what I've done or what I need to do. This can be harmful on both accounts.

When I wake up thinking of what I've done, I often feel guilt over the day before. When I wake up thinking about what I need to do, I often feel anxiety over the day to come.

Notice that in both of these cases, my prayers focus on *my* performance. When the focus is on only what I do (or don't do), that means I'm seeing life through the lens of legalism.

Legalism is the belief that the world hangs on what I do—that God and people love me based on how I perform, so I better get it right! This is the exact opposite of the gospel: God loves us not because of *what we do*, but rather *in spite of what we do*.

LEGALISM IS THE BELIEF THAT THE WORLD HANGS ON WHAT I DO—SO I BETTER GET IT RIGHT!

But legalism takes the unmerited love of God and bends it into something we earn. This seems to be the default setting for human beings. So our mornings begin, and then in a matter of a few words our day becomes all about us and not at all about God.

We will always wake up to some kind of prayer that makes the world about us—unless we create new habits of gospel-centered prayers. These are prayers that make the world less about us and more about God's love for us.

While I've been practicing some version of morning prayers my whole life, they radically changed when I got a smartphone. My smartphone exacerbates my tendency toward self-centered or legalistic morning prayers. Why? Because my phone is the portal through which the chaos of the world reaches my half-asleep heart.

Our phones—actually, their programmers—are happy to set our habits for us. They love to speak the first words of the day to us, and they usually do so through pesky notifications.

Now I want you to pause and emotionally prepare yourself for what I'm about to say. *I recommend you turn off notifications. All of them.* When I did that, it changed the tone and direction of my days.

Back when my notifications were turned on, I would wake to the "prayers" someone else wanted me to pray. If it was an early-morning work email with a task for me, I would begin the day wishing it could be done already. If it was a social media alert, I would start the day wishing my life could be a little more glamorous.

Each of these electronic nudges invited prayers of their own, usually prayers that framed my day in stress, envy, or cynicism—and they were all the more powerful because they were done by unconscious habit.

KNEELING MORNING PRAYERS

As I mentioned before, habits are something we do over and over without thinking about it. They shape our lives. And they typically form us more than we form them. That's why they are so powerful.

A *keystone habit* is a super-habit. By changing this one habit, we simultaneously change ten other habits. Beginning the day in kneeling prayer is such a keystone habit.

It took a terrible anxiety collapse to get me to think closely about what was happening in my heart each morning. I examined these moments, and I found that I was beginning the day by speaking words of my pride or fear into each day.

> A *KEYSTONE HABIT* IS A SUPER-HABIT.

I wanted to change that, but changing habits of the mind is immensely tricky.

Thoughts are slippery things. We can't grab them. Yet the Bible tells us to "take captive every thought to make it obedient to Christ" (2 Corinthians 10:5 NIV). So how could I frame the first words of my morning prayer in God's love for me?

For me, the first step was to use the automatic "do not disturb" function on my phone. (Often reprogramming our phones is a way to reprogram our thought life.)

Setting my phone to go to "do not disturb" at 9:00 p.m. and stay off until 8:00 a.m. meant only family and other select contacts could call me. This removed a thousand legalistic nudges during my morning prayer, but alone this was not enough.

The second step was to kneel. Often one of the only ways to take hold of your mind is to take hold of your body. As I knelt, my sleepy mind was shocked into the current moment. The cold floor might have helped, too.

There's nothing magic about kneeling. If you're unable to kneel, you can change your posture by turning your palms up, raising your head to the sky, or even breathing deeply. But getting the attention of your body is a good start to getting the attention of your soul.

Most days my morning prayer is very, very short. When I wake exhausted, often the first moment on my knees by the bed is a very quick, "Lord, have mercy." When I wake thinking about a project that needs way more hours than the day has, it's a slower pause for help: "Lord, I'm worried. Help me be like you and do good work that brings order to chaos." On those rare, glorious days when I wake rested, my prayer may be: “This is amazing! Thank you, Lord, for your care for me! Let me love others today like you love me.”

By uprooting the weeds of legalism in my life and attaching my prayers to God’s guiding trellis, my words gained power and purpose. Through God’s direction, I was speaking words of love into the world and recovering the two uses of prayer.

The first part of prayer names realities. This part is essential as it reminds us there are truths of the world: *God is good. We are loved. To be alive is beautiful. Gratitude is the way of happiness*. In this sense, prayer agrees with what God has created and reminds us of the way he designed the world.

The second part of prayer creates realities. Often this kind of prayer happens in the places where the order of creation has been broken: *Let me make something good of the world today. Comfort my friend as his mom battles cancer.*

With just two small shifts, your whole day can be reframed. Now it’s time to get to school.

KNEELING MIDDAY PRAYERS

Kneeling prayer at midday is a habit that can reframe your life at school.

Go back to the opening act of the Bible. The spotlight has just come on, and we find the Trinity on the stage, working together to create this beautiful and bizarre world. God is different parts blue-collar worker, artist, inventor, tinkerer, gardener, and entrepreneur. In all roles, he’s working with his hands, getting dirty, and calling this creative act *good*.

In fact, the Hebrew word that God says over and over is *tov*, which is something more than just good. It is something like *wow* or *whoa*—like the involuntary noise a crowd makes when an athlete does something spectacular.

While God created work and models what it should look like, we invert the purpose of work. God worked as service. He generously made the world for love of us. Instead of working as a way to love and serve others, we turn work into a way to be loved and be served by others.

Right now, school is your stage to showcase your work. So often at school we strive to hear the *tov* of teachers and classmates, not the *tov* of God.

Maybe you start your day on fire. A mix of caffeine, willpower, and fear of failure gets you through the first few classes and quizzes. Then the wheels begin to fall off. As you look at the remainder of the day, maybe you begin to think *I'm not good enough. I can't do it. People don't listen to me.*

All the feelings of legalism can return: *If I can't hack it in math class, what am I worth anyway?*

Kneeling prayer midday is a chance to reframe your day right as it is falling apart.

Ask a teacher with an open classroom, or find an empty locker room, and kneel in prayer. This is inevitably awkward. What if someone walks in? It's uncomfortable. But these are good discomforts. They remind us of our place and purpose on this planet—to serve God.

Again, if you're unable to kneel, there are other ways you can use your body to get the attention of your soul: turn your palms up, raise your head to the sky, breathe deeply, walk to a window, or step outside for a moment. Find a way to remind your body that it's time to pray.

My short midday prayers often have to do with a confession. Yours might, too. An impure thought. A snarky comment. A white lie to avoid getting in trouble. Pray for a friend you may have offended or a teacher that you had a bad attitude toward.

No matter what you do, this habit will interrupt things in the best of ways. By introducing this new habit, it puts a hook in each day—a place where the focus on self is snagged and disrupted. Then the rest of your school day can be turned toward someone else, whether a friend, teammate, teacher, or stranger.

KNEELING EVENING PRAYERS

Finally we come to the end of the day, the tenuous moment when we must take our hands off the wheel and let things rest. Maybe at this point we're frustrated because we had no time for free time. Or we're embarrassed because we squandered our free time watching TikTok videos.

The evening, then, can be a time of severe self-judgment. I often find myself lying in bed and facing the reality that I spent the whole day trying to justify my existence on earth. *Does any of it matter?*

That's a worrisome thought many of us can't turn off. Because of it, we want to tune everything out. And many of us do. A conversation with friends would help; but binging TV will let me tune out. Catching up on reading would be restful; but Instagram has some urgent notifications. I should talk with my parents; but talking is hard, and there's a podcast that everyone said I should listen to. There are more or less healthy ways to escape, but what we can't escape is the desire to escape.

The exhaustion of a day places us into a twilight where it isn't easy to make the right decisions. We're tired, and because our bodies and minds and souls are all bound up together, we have trouble making choices. The business world calls it "decision fatigue."

The evening can be a time of vulnerability. We haven't spent the day so much as the day has spent us. This is where an evening prayer can make one last and important turn of the day.

Perhaps it's once homework is done. We pause to pray, to purposefully frame the evening in rest instead of letting it slip into something else. Or perhaps we take seriously the act of going to bed and ask, *Am I going to browse my phone for some celebrity or scandal to bounce meaninglessly around in my brain? Or shall I walk intentionally toward the rest I know I need?*

It's impossible to find sleep if we believe it's up to us to keep the world spinning. Real rest comes when we thank God that we don't need to, because he does. So we kneel by the bed and focus on God's mercy and care for us at the end of the day.

We made it through another day. It doesn't matter whether we feel spiritual or not. It doesn't matter whether we know what to say or not. It doesn't matter whether we've said the same thing every night for a month or not. Small words have enormous impact.

REAL REST COMES WHEN WE THANK GOD THAT HE KEEPS THE WORLD SPINNING, NOT US.

Our words create new realities. One moment we can feel alone. The next we're united with God.

THINK ABOUT IT . . .

1. What is the first thing you do when you wake up? How does this shape your view of the day? Of yourself? Of God?

2. What pressure points during your day cause you to feel anxious, stress, guilt, or worry? How could prayer help you at these times?

3. If you could pick one time in your day to start practicing kneeling prayer, what time would you pick and why?

4. What is one small change you could make to improve your daily prayer life? Write it down and tell someone. Change happens with accountability.

DAILY HABIT 1

KNEELING PRAYER AT MORNING, MIDDAY, AND BEDTIME

THE HABIT AT A GLANCE

The world is made of words. Even small, repeated words have power. Regular, consistent prayer is one of the keystone habits of spiritual formation. By framing our day in the words of prayer, we frame the day in the love of God.

THREE WAYS TO START

Written prayers. You want to begin by having a morning, midday, and evening prayer. Here are three you might use (these are available to print on the Common Rule website):

- Morning. *Holy Spirit, may people see your presence in me. May this day be one where my words and actions reflect you. Amen.*
- Midday. *Jesus, I was made to join your work in the world. Please order the rest of my day in love for the people you put in my path. Amen.*
- Bedtime. *Father, I was made to rest in your love. May my body rest in sleep, and may my mind rest in your love. Amen.*

Alarms and reminders. After hearing a guy share for the fifth or sixth time how he wished he prayed more with his wife, a friend of mine picked up the guy's phone and told Siri to set an alarm to remind him to pray with his wife. It was funny, but also common sense. Use alarms if you're having trouble beginning the habit of prayer. For a long time, I had an alarm that went off at 1 p.m. each day to remind me to stop and pray.

Praying with the body. Kneeling is a great way to mark the moment with physicality and humility. If kneeling is challenging because you're in public, try gently turning up your palms and setting them on your knees, or walking to a window. The key is to change the posture of your body, but kneeling is best.

THREE CONSIDERATIONS

Communal prayers. Some friends of mine who practice the Common Rule at their offices use this as a chance to take a break and pray briefly together. Usually they find an empty conference room and take a five-minute break. My wife and I use evening prayer as a time to pray together before bed. Find some friends at school to consistently pray with you. You might be able to pray with a sibling or parent in the morning.

Variations. Because the habit of rhythmic prayer frames the day, consider praying at a specific time each day. If you ride the bus, consider praying as it pulls up. Maybe you can pray as you enter school as a way to transition your mind and heart into a posture of serving others.

Embracing repetition. Just because prayers are repetitive doesn't mean they're meaningless. Quite the opposite. Often these prayers form us over time because of their constant presence. Of course spontaneous prayers can be woven into your day, but building the trellis of repetitive prayer is a way to encourage more prayers to grow.

ONE MEAL WITH OTHERS

The believers studied what the apostles taught. They shared their lives together. They ate and prayed together.

ACTS 2:42 (NIRV)

When my wife and I left China to move back to the United States, we had almost no money. Our plan was for her to continue her career in philanthropy consulting. I would start law school. In other words, she would make money while I spent it.

We ended up in Washington DC, one of the most expensive housing markets in the United States. Not great planning. Our lives, and our wallets, were saved by a dear friend who invited us to live temporarily in a communal home called the Brethren House.

The way of the house was simple. We paid very little in rent, but we had to cook and clean and come to meals. A meal was served every evening, and we were expected to be there. Period. Once a week we had to make the meal. Once a week we cleaned up after it.

As you may expect, this was incredibly countercultural in the chaotic world of Georgetown Law School's power-schedules and appointments. I found myself jumping on the Metro to head home just as all my classmates were starting their next round of studying or meetings. But I had to "pay the rent" by coming to the table.

But instead of being frustrating, this was profoundly formational. In a matter of weeks, Lauren and I became remarkably close to the people in Brethren House. Because of the centrality of the dinner table in our daily schedules, our lives were calibrated for relationship, not loneliness.

Eating together isn't easy for many families—especially when busy teenagers are in the picture! Meals are often squeezed between other commitments or eaten on the run. To make this a habit, you must sync schedules, plan menus, and make a mutual priority of the meal.

The fact is, committing to the table means we have to rearrange our lives. That's the point. Our schedules need to be bent around creating community. The daily habit of a meal with others forms us in that direction.

Even if we fail constantly, which we are bound to do, the very act of trying to have one meal a day with others sets us firmly in a countercultural current. Studies show only half of American families eat dinner together.[1] Fewer than that do it around the table. The TV, not the table, has become the center of the family meal.

But while many families fail to enjoy a meal together, nine out of ten wish they did. And for good reason. Research shows that students who have family dinners get higher grades, have a lower risk of drug or alcohol abuse, are less likely to suffer symptoms of depression, and are more likely to graduate high school.[2] But it's not the food that accomplishes any of this. It's the time together—talking, telling stories, laughing, and doing life together. In other words, just sitting at the table and not talking won't do any good!

Cultivating this daily rhythm of one meal together, like most limits, brings more freedom than restriction. Sure, life can get crazy if you're part of a play, in the middle of a sports season, or cramming for finals. Missing a meal together isn't the end of the world. But the pattern of eating together, not the times you have to miss, is the key.

The idea is to have your schedule revolve around the table, not the table around your schedule.

MADE TO EAT

We can't live if we don't eat. At certain points in the day, we all have to stop and stuff something in our mouths.

I have friends who argue that food is simply fuel. While I agree we need to eat healthy in order to fill our stomachs with good fuel, I disagree with the idea that food is simply fuel. It's like saying our bodies are simply machines.

We're not machines; we're human beings. A people who are made to eat. Regularly. And with others.

The daily habit of one meal a day with others is a way of ordering our day around who we were created to be: dependent and communal human beings.

Just the fact that we are made to eat says volumes about who we are and who God is. We are not just hungry bodies, nor machines that simply need fuel. Our need for food says something profound about us. It says we need God, we need others, and we need the created world.

THE HABIT OF ONE MEAL A DAY WITH OTHERS IS A WAY OF ORDERING OUR DAY AROUND WHO WE WERE CREATED TO BE: DEPENDENT AND COMMUNAL HUMAN BEINGS.

The need to eat reveals our dependence on God. Perhaps one of the most significant differences between us and God is that we, unlike him, are dependent on things outside of ourselves. Food is our daily reminder of that. We were created to hunger in order to remind us that we are dependent on God's generosity.

The need to eat reveals our dependence on each other. From planting to harvesting to preparing food, one person can't do it all. We can't survive without each other's help. This distinguishes us from almost all other animals. Every snack we eat or meal we enjoy together signifies a vast web of dependence on our neighbors, which include farmers, harvesters, truckers, grocery workers, food manufacturers, and distribution warehouses.

The need to eat reveals our dependence on creation. We also live in a web of mutual sacrifice. Whether you're eating plants or meat, every single bite signifies a moment when something died to give *you* life. If you think about it, there's something distinctly Christlike about the fact that our ongoing daily life depends entirely on the sacrifice of other life on our behalf.

When we see food only as fuel, we lose some of this deeper meaning. We aren't grateful to God; we assume our right to food. We aren't grateful to each other; we take systems that provide our food for granted. We aren't grateful to creation; we consume the earth's food greedily and carelessly, as if the world were ours to trash instead of ours to steward and cultivate.

The daily habit of eating at least one meal with others is important precisely because it asks us to acknowledge our needs for food and for each other.

THE SCHOOL OF LOVE

Your home is not just a place where you spend a lot of time. It's a place of formation. For that reason, generations of Christians have described the household as "a school of love." The point of that phrase is to emphasize that most of the intangible things that make life worth living are learned at home. Or not.

The household is where we're first taught that the fundamental goal of life is to love each other. And the table is often the centerpiece of this formation.

Think through all the ways that the values of love are communicated over food. We serve each other. We clean up after each other. We take turns. We share. We fight and forgive. We praise and compliment. We express gratitude. We tell stories and ask questions. We listen. We hear each other pray.

Obviously, your parents set the tone for your household. But there's no reason you can't ask, "Do you think our family routine is too busy to allow for meals together or with friends and neighbors?"

If you'd like to begin this habit of eating a meal together, talk to your parents. Maybe you can have a family meeting where you share your ideas and insights. Reordering schedules to have meals together may take an immense amount of work, so everyone needs to be on board.

Another way to create "a school of love" is at your actual school. Most school lunch periods are thirty minutes or less. That's not a lot of time. But it doesn't take long to create a community. Committing to eat at the same table with the same people every day helps make stronger connections. It's a time when you can talk and support each other. Your day can be refreshed and re-energized.

Maybe you organize a group of friends from church to eat together or perhaps you invite the people you hang with at school. However you do it, gather your group and start eating together. Then see what happens.

Not only will your relationships grow in love, but the amazing thing about making the table the center of gravity is the way it begins to pull others into its orbit.

MEAL AS MISSION

We live in a culture where most people resist talking about or hearing the truth of the gospel. What's more, many of the people in our lives *can't* hear it because we no longer share a common vocabulary. *Does truth exist? What can be called good? How do we show love?*

But that is okay. God is not alarmed. Our modern world is not a barrier to evangelism, it is simply the place of evangelism.[3] One of the reasons I'm so compelled by the life of habit is that I see habits as a way for light to shine in an age of darkness.

Cultivating a life of habits means our ordinary ways of living stand out in the culture, dancing like candles in the night. As Madeleine L'Engle once wrote, "We draw people to Christ not by loudly discrediting what they believe . . . but by showing them a light that is so lovely that they want with all their hearts to know the source of it."[4]

In this age, eating may be our best chance for evangelism. More Americans regularly eat alone now than ever before. Maybe you've seen that in your school, or you have a neighbor or friend who ends up alone most evenings.

Food is meant to bind us to God, neighbor, and creation. But we live in a culture where our eating habits keep us apart and increase our isolation. The best way to understand the Common Rule habit of one meal a day with others is to see it as a way of turning on the light of presence in a dark culture of loneliness.

Like all of the habits, the point is to adopt the rhythms of the gospel into our daily lives and to have those rhythms become a blessing to us and our neighbors.

The central promise of salvation is that because of the death and resurrection of Jesus, God and people will rejoice. The end of the world culminates not in the clouds but in a *feast* (see Revelation 19:6-9). At the wedding supper of the Lamb, the divine presence is restored to us over a table of food.

Remember that we don't get invited to the table because of anything we've done. We get invited because of what Jesus has done. This is why Christians regularly come to the Communion table to feast on the body and blood of Christ. It is a reminder that because of Christ, we will commune with God again over food.

THE POINT IS TO ADOPT THE RHYTHMS OF THE GOSPEL INTO OUR DAILY LIVES AND TO HAVE THOSE RHYTHMS BECOME A BLESSING TO US AND OUR NEIGHBORS.

To find each other over food each day is to plant and cultivate the culture of communion in our homes, schools, and neighborhoods. So invite those around you to come. Then let us eat!

THINK ABOUT IT . . .

1. How would you describe your daily meal routine? Is community, planning, or prayer involved? How?

2. Have you ever thought about the spirituality of eating? What does our need to eat show us about our dependence on God, creation, and others?

3. When was the last time you invited someone outside your friend group to eat lunch with you? Has your family ever invited a neighbor over for dinner? What happened?

4. How could meals with others be a starting point for evangelism or outreach to others in need? Who in your life could you extend an invitation to?

DAILY HABIT 2

ONE MEAL WITH OTHERS

THE HABIT AT A GLANCE

We were made to eat. The habit of making time for one communal meal each day forces us to organize our schedules and our space around food and one other.

THREE WAYS TO START

Family meals. Getting into the rhythm of a family breakfast or dinner may be the best way to start. Talk to your parents and siblings about which meal works best for your family. Try to make it the anchor of your schedule.

School lunch. Establishing a regular group to eat with can be a great way to create a meaningful break in the school day as well as an opportunity to build relationships. Whether there's just two of you or ten, agree on where to meet for lunch. Then look for new students or students who sit by themselves to join you. You might even invite the new person for a one-on-one meal before introducing them to the group.

Eat communally while alone. If you wish you had a family willing to do meals together or friends at school to eat with, this could be a hard chapter for you to read. I want you to know that there will be a day all loneliness is gone forever. If you find yourself alone, talk to God. His spirit is always with you. Maybe you can sit at a new table at school without a phone or headphones—in a way that invites conversation and new friendships.

EATING TOGETHER FEEDS YOUR BODY AND YOUR SOUL.

THREE CONSIDERATIONS

Creating space. Space matters. If you're at home, work with your parents to create an inviting table. You want a space that draws everyone in. This can be as simple as helping clear homework off the table, and then helping set the table before mealtime.

The table as formation. Some of the ways my family tries to make mealtimes intentionally relational is by lighting a candle. Then we give God thanks, using prayers everyone knows so we can take turns saying them. We also have come up with regular questions to ask and answer. In the morning, ours are "What are you hoping for today?" and "What are you not looking forward to today?" At dinner, it's "One good thing, one bad thing, one funny thing." With a group of friends, I've always appreciated the "One Conversation Rule." That means, at some point in the meal, everyone has a single conversation together instead of lots of side conversations.

Turning meals inside out. I have a friend who makes a simple homemade pizza meal every Friday. The prep is low, and no one has to think hard. Then his family invites over someone new. This is a great way to take the family rhythm of dinner and extend it to a neighbor or friend. Another way is to have your family eat in your front yard or on your front porch instead of your backyard—and then be ready to welcome a neighbor to join you!

DAILY HABIT 3

ONE HOUR WITH PHONE OFF

Look, God's home is now among his people! He will live with them.

A LOUD SHOUT FROM THE THRONE (REVELATION 21:3)

Has this ever happened to you?

You're talking with your mom. She's giving you the rundown of her day—the meetings, the errands, the rides your little brother needs. You're in the same room with her, but you're really not there.

A friend has messaged you. Something is trending. Someone commented on your post. You remember you need to get back to your history project group with ideas for the project—

"So what do you think?" she says.

You have zero idea what your mom has been saying, because you've subconsciously picked up your phone and begun scrolling through notifications. Statistics show many teens receive nearly 250 notifications on their phones every day. Some get as many as 5,000 in twenty-four hours![1]

Even though I don't receive nearly that many notifications because I've changed my settings, I'm still guilty of this all the time. I act like I'm talking to someone but my attention is elsewhere, which basically makes me a liar.

I've lied to the person about where my presence is, and I've lied to myself about how many ways I can split my presence and still be present. I've tried to be two places at once, and as a result, I'm no place.

This is the core struggle of the smartphone. It's amazing because it allows us to communicate our presence across time and space, but it's dangerous for the very same reason. It can fracture our presence across time and space until we become absent in the moment.

> SMARTPHONES CAN FRACTURE OUR PRESENCE ACROSS TIME AND SPACE UNTIL WE BECOME ABSENT IN THE MOMENT.

We don't mean to live lives of absence. But without meaningful habits to resist this technology, smartphones are impossible not to look at. They're designed that way. The buzz in our pocket or chime of a notification releases the hormone *dopamine* in our brains. This is the same brain chemical that's released when we take a delicious bite of food, have a big laugh with a friend, or even do drugs.[2] And that makes our phones addictive.

If we do nothing, we're sure to live a life of addicted, fractured presence. And that's not much of a life at all, because presence is the essence of life itself.

PRESENCE AS LIFE

Presence is at the heart of who we are, because presence is at the core of our relationship with God. From creation to salvation, the story of the Bible is fundamentally a story of presence.

The Garden of Eden was paradise because the presence of God was there. God was with Adam and Eve, until their sin broke the bliss of that presence. After eating the fruit, Adam and Eve suddenly wanted to cover themselves and hide. This is the hallmark of life as we know it now. We hide from each other, and we hide from God.

Sin has turned a people meant for presence into a people of absence.

Fortunately the story of the Bible doesn't end in Genesis. God spends the rest of the story accompanying his people. First, he leads them through deserts and wildernesses. He appears in clouds of smoke and burning bushes. He finds them in midnight dreams and pillars of fire. He manifests his presence on a mountain, in a tabernacle, and in a temple. The Israelites are known as God's people because of one thing: God's presence is among them.

This culminates in the salvation story of the New Testament. Jesus is called *Emmanuel*, which means "God *with* us." That's not an accident. It's a powerful truth.

Jesus came to bridge the divide between God and people so we could be together again. He did this through his death and resurrection. By atoning for our sins on the cross and defeating death through his resurrection, he cleared the path for the presence of God to once again become the cornerstone of our reality. Now, like the Israelites, a Christ follower is defined by "God with us." But instead of a pillar of fire, we follow the Holy Spirit who lives in us (see 1 Corinthians 6:19).

That is why, for a Christian, presence is the heart of everything.

FRACTURED PRESENCE

When we try to be present everywhere, we end up being fully present nowhere. But when we embrace the reality of our ability to be present only in one place, we find the deep joy of being fully present somewhere.

This is why we need to be attentive to our smartphone habits. The smartphone is a tool that enables many things, but it will never multiply our presence. When we try to use it that way, it only brings our absence. For example: checking texts during a meal, taking a call while in the middle of a conversation, posting about a conflict instead of talking to someone about it, taking videos of people in distress instead of helping them, capturing a picture of someone who doesn't know it, shooting a video of a concert instead of enjoying the moment live. These are all examples of fractured presence, and they do real harm—both to us and our neighbors. This absence is the cause of much brokenness in the world.

The goal of resisting absence is to give others our presence—our *attention*. And our attention is a precious and limited commodity. We have to ask ourselves: What is worthy of our attention?

Our phones are carefully designed to attract our attention and then sell our attention to advertisers. There is a powerful monetary incentive that frames the functionality of all our devices. Our phones learn our preferences and curate ads and other content to meet our desires. This doesn't necessarily make them evil capitalistic machines, but it certainly means they aren't neutral. It also means we have to work hard to control them, because they won't control themselves and they would love to control us.

Many teens say they're on their phone "all the time." That's not quite true. But research shows teens spend an average of five hours to seven-and-a-half hours a day on their phones. And that doesn't count time spent for schoolwork.[3]

All that phone time, especially on social media, can have negative effects. Studies say heavy smartphone use and media multitasking result in chronic sleep deprivation, poor academic performance, negative body image, and increased mental distress—including depression, anxiety, and suicidal thoughts.[4]

Experts have found that limiting phone time to about one hour a day helps anxious teens' mental health.[5] One hour. For many of us, that's not practical or possible (although it would be freeing).

Instead of going to that extreme—which *has* proven to help teens struggling with body image and mental health issues—I suggest making the Common Rule habit to turn off your phone for an hour a day. Sounds reasonable, right?

So try it right now. Just as an experiment. I dare you. Wait until your phone is totally off before you read the next paragraph.

First of all, you almost certainly just got distracted by a few notifications on the way to turning it off. If you're back, I'm impressed if it took you less than five minutes.

Second, now that your phone is off, you probably notice a palpable feeling of aloneness—like someone walked out of a room. You may even feel a tinge of anxiety or dread.

Many of us view our phones as an extension of ourselves. If we turn off our phones, that means we cut off the possibility of our presence from others. We can't reach out or be reached. This is exactly what is scary, and it's exactly why we should be turning off our phones every day as a habit.

The goal is to regularly cut off the ability to be reached by everyone and anyone, so that within those limits we can be fully present to someone.

FORMING A LIFE OF PRESENCE

My hour with my phone off starts shortly after I get home from work. This is when I reengage with my kids and my wife.

Look at your schedule to determine a consistent time for you to turn off your phone. Maybe it's when you gather for dinner with your family. That can be the perfect time for no phone access so you can give your attention to those around the table.

Maybe it's when you're doing homework or working on a project. Many teens listen to music or have videos playing on their phones while they're doing homework. But with these outside distractions, we're never able to experience the intense pleasure that comes from doing focused work on one important task—often referred to as *deep work* or *flow*.[6]

This is the state where real work happens, and it never happens in the presence of a phone. I've found that when I don't silence other distractions and focus on one thing, a three-hour task can turn into a three-day sprawling project littered with interruptions.

In the age of smartphones, the ability to purposefully resist distraction is becoming the single most important skill for success. Turning off our phone helps us do better work more quickly.

What's more, by freeing up hours in our day, we create time to serve our neighbor. And service can be expressed in all sorts of ways. Listening to a friend at school. Vacuuming the house without being asked. Volunteering at children's church. Rolling the trash to the curb for an elderly neighbor.

By giving our undivided attention to the people around us, we're better able to see their needs. There is no love of neighbor outside of attention to neighbor. Therefore, having periods of keeping your phone off is a keystone habit for loving neighbors.

IN THE AGE OF SMARTPHONES, THE ABILITY TO PURPOSEFULLY RESIST DISTRACTION IS BECOMING THE SINGLE MOST IMPORTANT SKILL FOR SUCCESS. TURNING OFF OUR PHONE HELPS US DO BETTER WORK MORE QUICKLY.

Turning off your phone also creates *silence*. I was a couple of months into my anxiety crash when I came across Blaise Pascal's famous quote: "All of man's problems stem from his inability to sit quietly in a room alone."

When I read those words, I felt a rush of panic come over me. *Why was I afraid?* Because I knew it to be devastatingly true.

The tragic irony when it comes to a troubled emotional life is that distraction functions both as one of the best quick fixes and as one of the roots of the problem. To sit peacefully in silence requires knowing our soul, knowing who we really are, and being fundamentally at peace with that. This is exactly why we avoid it; we don't know who we really are. Or if we do, we're terrified of ourselves. Silence confronts us with that fact, so we will do anything to avoid it.

In the couple of years after reading the Pascal quote, I realized that I needed to confront my fear of silence. So I decided to go to a local retreat center for a day of silence. The first time I walked into the room and the retreat leader told us that we were going to begin with twenty minutes of group silence, I was genuinely afraid.

But I survived.

Anything that is good for you initially hurts. Silence is the same. By the end of my first day of silence, it seemed as if the silence itself had begun to loosen the tangled knots of my heart.

Years later, I see that was exactly what happened, because constant distraction and inattention are what tied me up in knots in the first place.

Maybe you're in the same place as I was.

Silence begins as a personal practice, but it ends as a public virtue. Just think of social media. When we can't answer the question of who we are in silence, we can't answer it in public either. Our insecurities spill out in the form of snarky comments, ranting arguments, or photos that display our "best life." None of these are our true self. In fact, very few people share their true self over social media because that kind of transparency is truly frightening.

By cultivating inner rhythms of silence, we become attentive to God's love for us and for the world, to our conscience, and to our neighbor's need. But many of us can't "hear" any of this—mostly because we're never quiet.

Ultimately, we can use our phone one way and it fuels the life of love and presence we long for. Use our phone another way and it robs us of everything we were made for.

And don't forget your phone isn't neutral. You can't use it the right way without habits that protect you from the wrong way.

This is why we must cultivate habits that resist absence, because we were made for presence. Cultivating the daily habit of turning off your phone for an hour is a keystone habit that can change the way you think about your phone and spark new daily routines that usher in a life of presence.

Okay, you can turn your phone back on now.

THINK ABOUT IT . . .

1. How would you rate your relationship with your phone on a scale of 1-10?

2. Did you turn off your phone while reading this chapter? How did that make you feel? If you didn't, how do you think turning off your phone would affect you?

3. Have you ever thought about how loving God and others depends on being present? How do you see phone usage affecting your presence?

4. How often is your phone out of reach? Think about where your phone is when you're at school, eating dinner, hanging with friends, or sleeping. Why do you keep it where you do, and what does that say about how you view the importance of your phone?

5. If you were to pick an hour each day to have your phone off, when would it be? If you were to do this for a month straight, what do you think would happen?

DAILY HABIT 3

ONE HOUR WITH PHONE OFF

THE HABIT AT A GLANCE

We were made for presence. Often our phones are the cause of our absence from others. To be two places at a time is to be no place at all.

Turning off our phone for an hour a day is a way to turn our gaze from down at a screen to *up*—toward our friends, family, neighbors, fellow students, and God. Our habits of attention are habits of love. To resist absence is to love our neighbor.

THREE WAYS TO START

Hour at home. I find that having the same hour every day goes a long way toward creating a rhythm of presence at home. In my house, somewhere around 6:30 and 7:30 p.m. is the best time for phones to be off for conversation, play, and presence.

Hour at school**.** Choose a time when you need to concentrate or get creative work done.

Hour for silence. You may choose the first or last hour of your day to turn off your phone. This can create meaningful space for solitude and silence. Consider using "Do Not Disturb" or a similar setting on your phone to set up regular phone-free hours. Better yet, put your phone to bed before you go to sleep and don't turn it on right away when you wake up.

THREE CONSIDERATIONS

The art of communication. So much is solved by communicating well. Tell your friends about your hour with your phone off. If you have a demanding social life that makes an hour without your phone seem impossible, think hard about whether that is really the case. Often it's just hard, not impossible. Especially if you're afraid about communicating what you're doing by following these Common Rule habits. But telling other people about your desire to change your habits is important. Who knows, maybe your friends will want to join you in this adventure.

Mastering devices. Beyond turning off your phone, you can use settings to shape your phone into being a device that is more likely to communicate your presence instead of divide your presence. I suggest turning off all notifications. Then over a week, turn back on the ones you truly miss. Also use voice controls whenever possible. This will keep you from opening the phone and then getting distracted by ten things when you only needed to do one thing.

A place for phones. Whether at school or home, consider having a place for your phone. Set up a charger, put your phone there, and leave it. At work I keep mine where I can't reach it or see it, so I can be present and purposeful. At home I put it up on the mantel or in my dresser drawer. Consider asking your parents to have a charging station near the front door, so when your friends come over you can offer a place where they can leave their phones. Having a place for phones goes a long way toward controlling your phone instead of it controlling you.

THE SMARTPHONE IS A TOOL THAT ENABLES MANY THINGS, BUT IT WILL NEVER MULTIPLY OUR PRESENCE.

DAILY HABIT 4

SCRIPTURE BEFORE PHONE

For the word of God is alive and powerful. It is sharper than the sharpest two-edged sword, cutting between soul and spirit, between joint and marrow. It exposes our innermost thoughts and desires.
HEBREWS 4:12

Social media has always been a great temptation for me because I'm a vain person. I've never been able to sign on to social media without my mind and heart immediately beginning to spin: *How many followers or likes do I have? Why does so-and-so have more when she always posts stupid kid stuff? Wait, when did he get promoted? Is his new title better than mine?*

My identity spiral rages as I get pulled in to others' posts and become aware of my lack of social impact.

During some points in my life, I would wake up, roll over, pick up my phone, and start scrolling. Many times I would look at work emails. Other times I would get my blood boiling by reading news alerts about political dealings. And, of course, I would sometimes go onto social media. The abyss of my smartphone consumed me. And I'm not alone.

More than 70 percent of teens say they often or sometimes grab their phone to check for messages and notifications *as soon as* they wake up.[1]

By starting our morning facing a screen, we're allowing our smartphones to set the tone for the day. After finding myself caught in this trap for years, I realized something deeper was happening. It was like my head was asking my phone a very practical question: *What do I need to do today?*

And in the same moment, under the surface, my heart was asking my phone a much more profound question: *Who do I need to become today?*

FRACTURED, NOT REFLECTIVE IDENTITY

Who am I? And who am I becoming? These are the questions our morning routines inevitably ask and answer for us. No words except the words of Scripture can accurately reply to these questions.

> WE DO NOT KNOW WHO WE ARE APART FROM THE GOD WHO MADE US, AND WE DO NOT KNOW WHO WE ARE BECOMING APART FROM THE GOD WHO IS RENEWING US.

The story of Scripture is clear. We do not know who we are apart from the God who made us, and we do not know who we are becoming apart from the God who is renewing us.

We long to know who we are. We daydream about versions of ourselves that we hope to become. But apart from Jesus we can do neither of these things.

Picture a broken mirror. Shards of glass litter the ground. That's what we humans are—broken reflectors. Alone we reflect a small piece of who God is. Together and redeemed by Christ, we fully can reflect him.

This means we can't know who we are by looking deep inside, discovering our true identity, and then mustering up all our effort and willpower to become that person. That is not how it works *at all*.

If we look inside ourselves, we often find a self in conflict. This is because we are created in the image of God, but we are fallen. Good and evil war within us.

This isn't a new phenomenon. The apostle Paul, the greatest missionary of all time and author of much of the New Testament, faced the same inward battle. In Romans 7:19-20 he writes, "For I do not do the good I want to do, but the evil I do not want to do—this I keep on doing. Now if I do what I do not want to do, it is no longer I who do it, but it is sin living in me that does it" (NIV).

So what did Paul do? Was he able to discover his true self? Yes, but *not* by turning within. He turned to Jesus. And we can do the same.

Paul went from being frustrated at his inner conflict and calling himself a "wretched man" in need of rescue, to thanking God for delivering him through Jesus Christ (see Romans 7:24-25 NIV).

Like Paul, we have different versions of ourselves that fight against each other. There are versions of ourselves we think we should be, versions our parents think we should be, versions our coaches and teachers think we should be, versions our culture urges us to be—and the list goes on.

This means the way we guide our formation is not by looking in and choosing our favorite identity; it is actually by looking out. Because we are little mirrors made to reflect big things, our internal sense of identity actually ends up reflecting the many different things we've spent our life looking at, whether good or not.

We can't become *ourselves* by ourselves. The way we discover ourselves is by staring at someone else.

This can be dangerous if we look to another person for identity, such as a boyfriend, girlfriend, friend on social media, or influencer. Staring at another broken shard of glass only makes us more broken.

But when we turn our eyes toward Jesus, we finally see the kind of person we were made to be. We are children of the King, perfectly loved—not because that's "who we are," but because that's who he is making us.

In his death and resurrection, Jesus gave us his place in the universe. We're heirs to the King of the new heavens and the new earth. Our most true sense of identity is found only in the story of who we are becoming, and that story is found in the words of the Bible.

We become ourselves only by gazing on that story. But every morning there are other stories competing for our identity. The Common Rule habit of Scripture before phone is intended to cultivate the habit of resisting those stories and embracing the true story.

SOCIAL ENVY AND VANITY

Social media is filled with anything but true stories. It's chock-full of our *best life*, not our *real life*. For that reason, abandoning my Facebook and deleting Instagram helped me to carry on life without the personal struggles and troubles I experienced on social media. I was pleasantly aloof.

So it was the height of irony that in initial calls with my publisher about *The Common Rule*, this conversation happened:

Publisher: One of the important parts of marketing this book will be having an active social media presence.

Me: Oh. [long pause] Like—um. How active do you mean when you say active?

Publisher: Consistency is better than volume, but maybe a couple tweets a day and one or two Facebook posts a day.

Me (in a silent thought bubble): *Have you even read what my book is about?*

But I was easily convinced that some social media activity would be a great way to get the Common Rule habits into the lives of more people. The missional impulse in me told me that's where my neighbors are who need the love of God. If I wanted to speak love to the world, social media would be one way to have the world's ear. I needed to learn to speak that language, just as I needed to learn Mandarin to be a missionary to China.

Then I began to wonder, *How can I stay just far enough from the world to love it well? How can I be* in *the realms of social media but not* of *these realms?* I didn't want to fall back into the self-doubt and diminished self-worth that social media had created in me in the past.

So like most important questions in my life, this required careful and communal thinking—and a lot of failure—before I found the answers. My friends helped me think through some simple practices to keep social media in its proper place. Here are some things I have learned.

First, I try to open a site only when I need to post or respond. I don't go on social media because I'm bored or have a spare moment. Those spare moments are reserved for staring at walls, which is infinitely more useful. Therefore, I schedule time once in the morning, once in the early afternoon, and once in the evening to put out content that I think will help someone or to engage with someone who is responding in a healthy way.

Second, I avoid unplanned scrolling. Unplanned scrolling usually means I'm hungry for something to catch my eye—and plenty of strange, dark, and bizarre things are happy to catch the eye on social media. Planned scrolling can be very different. But in general, I believe we should be wary of the flicking thumb motion. A restless thumb often correlates to a restless heart.

Third, I turn off notifications. There is no good reason I (or any human being) need to know in real time who is liking my posts when and how much. There are some useful purposes for these stats, but not in each and every moment.

Fourth, I don't use social media in bed. Beds are most useful for rest. Social media is many things, but it is not a place of rest—even though there are colossal temptations to use it for both. Mixing social media and bed tempts me to confuse these lines. The best way to win this fight: throw the phone out of the bed.

Fifth, when I come across mean things said about me or someone I love, I employ a timeless strategy that parents use with their three-year-olds: ignore the temper tantrum. Words are not nearly as useful as silence in this case. Social media has its purpose, but venting anger is not one of them.

Sixth, I set a timer on apps I may need to use but don't want to get lost in scrolling. Most phones now have this feature, and it's a great nudge to come back to real life.

I fail at all of these practices regularly, but that doesn't mean the rules aren't good, I'm just not. I still struggle with envy. I can list people I know with more followers than I have. Sometimes I stand over a screen, hovering with a finger while I say to myself, *Do not open this just to check for likes*. Then I fail and do it.

The more I use social media, however, the more I realize the great danger is not in simply overusing social media, it is in *living through* social media. The problem is not so much the way it wastes time, it is the way it *frames* time. Without limits on our use of social media, we begin to see our whole life through it.

In our modern era, a popular saying goes, "If you don't post about it, it didn't really happen." By following these sentiments, we end up seeing our whole day as a potential post. We look around, wondering what is worth taking a picture of. We listen to every conversation for a catchy quote, instead of trying to understand the human being who is talking. We avoid disagreement in public, yet we express our most ardent emotions in carefully crafted posts.

This is no way to live. In fact, it's a miserable way to live. There is no love of neighbor in it, and there is no solution for it outside of becoming formed in the love story of Scripture.

If we wake every morning to social media, we will be formed in its lens on life and all the envy, bullying, and self-righteousness that goes with that. Fortunately, there's a different way.

The Bible tells a story of *us*—not as people who were made to see and be seen or judge and be judged, but as children who were made to love and be loved. Only when we feel that in our bones can we use social media to love neighbors instead of trying to get their love.

ELECTION LOSS WITHOUT IDENTITY LOSS

As a child, I woke up expecting to find my dad reading in his study every morning. Usually it was his Bible. I'm sure he didn't do it every day. But my memories of him in the morning are seeing him at his desk with his Bible and a notebook. I actually still have his Bible.

Recently, I flipped open that Bible and landed in Colossians. Written at the start of these chapters were a series of dates: On January 7, 2002, he read chapter one. On January 8, he read chapter two. And so on.

Looking back, these were months after he lost the Virginia governor's race. My dad was a politician for fifteen years during my upbringing. That race, his biggest race, was the only one he ever lost.

I can still remember crying myself to sleep on November 6, 2001, after the initial votes were counted. I was disappointed (admittedly because I had really wanted to live in the governor's mansion and have my own bodyguard).

I'm sure my dad was disappointed, too. Yet the first thing he did on the morning after that loss was to make us pancakes and tell us what he'd read in the Bible that morning. He was excited. He was wondering what was next for him. And he was okay with not being governor because he knew who he was.

I think my dad managed to keep a stable identity through a roller coaster of political successes and failures due to his habit of looking each morning to God's love before he turned to look at the world.

For some unexplainable reason, I didn't follow my dad's example in my morning routine when I became an adult. Instead of immediately turning to God's Word, I turned to emails, political posts, and social media.

Then during the summer of 2016, I picked up a commentary on Isaiah that a former professor had given me years before. I hadn't read Isaiah for ages, so I decided to browse it.

I began to make Isaiah my morning reading, not my smartphone. Quickly, I fell headlong into a very, very different story of what was going on. It was a story of a God who loves and defends the poor and the vulnerable, a God who's righteously angry over injustice while remaining tender to both the victims and the perpetrators of that injustice.

Reading Isaiah began to ease me away from the dangerous mindsets of thinking *what do I need to do* or *what do I need to become* at the start of my day. Isaiah helped me understand that I wasn't the one who knew what to do. Isaiah turned my attention to a just and merciful God who avenges all injustice and gives his people peace.

Maybe most importantly, Isaiah reminded me of the power and purpose of God's Word in my life. In Isaiah 55:11 the prophet wrote these words given to him by God: "My word that goes out from my mouth: It will not return to me empty, but will accomplish what I desire and achieve the purpose for which I sent it" (NIV).

God's Word always accomplishes its purpose. Not just sometimes. Always. For that reason alone, it's a habit worth cultivating every morning. The Bible reminds us who God is and who we are in him.

THE BIBLE REMINDS US WHO GOD IS AND WHO WE ARE IN HIM. FOR THAT REASON ALONE, IT'S A HABIT WORTH CULTIVATING EVERY MORNING.

And once you know who you are in God, you can turn to the world in love. If you don't understand who you are in God, you'll turn to the world looking for love. As a result, much of our identity hinges on the proper ordering.

WAKING AS A CHILD OF THE KING

There's something else about the pages in Colossians that I randomly flipped to in my dad's Bible. Each of these dates had the annotation "w/Justin."

January 7, 8, and 9—the very days I happened to open to—were mornings my dad and I spent together in the winter of 2002.

I was a senior in high school. Every morning he would wake me and invite me to read the Bible with him before school.

Before you get the wrong picture, I wasn't the model Christian high schooler. I had a mass of warring identities. I was trying to figure out which friend, which party, which drinking game, which girl, which grade, and which band would give me the identity I needed in order to feel good about myself.

It was during that time—precisely when I seemed the least receptive to his parenting—that my dad was most vigilant about inviting me to his study in the morning to pray. And I joined him because I knew he had the stable identity that I longed for. Waking wasn't easy. I wasn't always happy to be there and often nodded off during prayer. But I was there.

All these years later, I can't recall a single passage of Scripture we read together. But I do remember something. Something really important.

What I remember is having a dad who wanted to be with me.

What I remember is reading together about a God who wants to be with us.

Over the course of many mornings, by habit, my dad taught me that I was his and that we were God's. No matter what went on in the world, we were both children, dearly loved.

Each morning presents us with these questions: *Who am I? And who am I becoming?* Each morning, the Scriptures answer the same, with God saying, "You are my child, and you are becoming like me." That is something to stand the day on.

We can't become ourselves by looking inward, and we can't become ourselves by staring at our strange reflections in a screen. We have to look into the Word. Like the apostle Peter said, "Lord, to whom would we go? You have the words that give eternal life" (John 6:68).

Cultivating the habit of Scripture before phone means looking in the right place to ask who you are. You open the Bible, and you find you are with your Dad. You find your name written on its pages. You find you are loved. Then you begin to reflect that love, just as you were made to.

THINK ABOUT IT . . .

1. What's the first thing you do each morning? What's the first thing you do on your phone each morning? How does this practice shape your day?

2. If the Bible were a person, how would you describe your relationship? (Select one.)

   - ○ A teacher you're afraid of.
   - ○ A friend you chat with all the time.
   - ○ An old friend you don't talk to anymore.
   - ○ A person you respect but don't know well.

3. Reading Scripture before phone is intended to push your phone out of your morning routine. If you were to try this habit, how might that rearrange your morning? If mornings aren't best for you, what time of day could you practice this habit?

4. If you can stand the irony, how would using an audio Bible app or reading plan app help you practice the heart of Scripture before phone? If you think it would help, choose one (maybe invite friends to join you) and start.

___

___

___

DAILY HABIT 4

SCRIPTURE BEFORE PHONE

THE HABIT AT A GLANCE

Refusing to check your phone until you read Scripture is a way of replacing the question "What do I need to do today?" with a better one: "Who am I and who am I becoming?"

This habit isn't about reading the entire book of Jeremiah—the longest book in the Bible at nearly 33,000 words—at one time. It's about starting your day by reading a chapter, a passage, or a couple verses. Anything that gets you into God's Word.

Daily reading of Scripture helps us resist the anxiety of emails, the anger of news, and the envy of social media. Instead it forms us daily in our true identity as children of the King.

THREE WAYS TO START

Reading plans. Getting a daily devotional is a great way to start these daily readings. But you can always grab a Bible and get reading! Here are a few suggestions for the next month:

- *Psalms.* Whether you go through them in order or otherwise, reading a morning psalm is always a great place to start.
- *Matthew.* The Gospel of Matthew has twenty-eight chapters. Try reading one each morning for a month.
- *Romans.* The book of Romans has sixteen chapters, so read half a chapter each morning for a month.

Daily Bible apps. I prefer reading a printed Bible because of the way tactile engagement focuses my mind. But I often find a Bible or prayer app on my phone very useful if I'm traveling or if I have to get out of the house early. The Daily Prayer app is a great place to start. You can even have apps read the Bible to you if you're an auditory learner.

Breakfast routine. The main purpose of this habit is simply to get your phone out of your morning routine. Try starting with a week of leaving your phone alone for the first hour of each morning. Breakfast and Scripture. Then add journaling, meditating, other readings, or exercising to begin your day.

THREE CONSIDERATIONS

Seasons. Sometimes school projects or studying for finals require attention first thing in the morning. I have seasons like that, when a project is important enough or around-the-clock enough that I need to check on things early each morning. If you're in a busy season, cut yourself some slack. Maybe read a psalm and jump back into checking on assignments.

Long study. Every follower of Jesus can study the Bible in depth. But if you're not a vocational minister or on a weekend retreat, you're likely not going to study the Bible in depth every single day. That's okay. Let longer times of reading a book or commentary grow out of reading your Bible regularly (not get in the way of it). Remember, these habits are a trellis that allows growth. Similarly, short daily readings build a foundation for longer and deeper study.

REPLACE THE QUESTION "WHAT DO I NEED TO DO TODAY?" WITH A BETTER ONE: "WHO AM I AND WHO AM I BECOMING?"

Journaling. Journaling is a keystone habit—that is, it changes everything else in your life. If you make a habit of filling up one page—while you read or pray or are silent, and before picking up your phone—your life will change.

WEEKLY HABIT 1

ONE HOUR OF CONVERSATION WITH A FRIEND

> *No longer do I call you servants, for the servant does not know what his master is doing; but I have called you friends, for all that I have heard from my Father I have made known to you.*
>
> JESUS (JOHN 15:15 ESV)

It was fall. I was sitting in my living room with a close friend when I got a call. Someone we both knew had become addicted to prescription drugs.

This was scary, not just because we hear about these kinds of problems often, but because people seem so "normal" before we learn their terrible secrets. We all seem to have a capacity to make ourselves appear okay, while hiding something that slowly kills us from the inside out.

As we sat there in shock and sadness, we did not say, "How could this happen?" or "What are the gory details?"

Something much more personal floated about the room. It was an unspoken question: *Is there anything you aren't telling me?*

This question goes either unasked or unanswered in so many lives that collapse. But if honestly asked and honestly answered, this question can turn lives around.

So that's what we asked each other. And the answer we both gave was, "No, you know everything."

The weekly habit of an hour of conversation is meant to cultivate this kind of life—where you know and are known by those closest to you.

MADE FOR FRIENDSHIP

One of the unique beliefs of the Christian faith is that God is three persons in one God. Among the many implications of the Trinity (Father, Son, and Holy Spirit), my favorite is that God is a *fellowship*. That means we are made in the image of fellowship.

This tells a very different story from what we read in science books. It means we didn't come from chaos. We aren't simply accidental life created from random circumstance. We also did not come forth from loneliness, as if a needy god needed lesser beings to sing its praises. We came from friendship.

Everything in the universe has its roots in friendship. The longing to be in right relationship with other people and with God is at the heart of every molecule in existence—and most powerfully in our own hearts.

We can't be happy without knowing and being known, because that's the image of the triune friendship we were made in. This explains why there is only one time in the creation story when God says the words "not good," and it is when the man is alone (Genesis 2:18). Everything else that comes before is proclaimed as "good."

God looked at the molecule of twin hydrogen plus oxygen—Good! The arctic coastline—Good! The acai palm tree—Good! The antelope—Good! But something was not good about the pinnacle of all creation, man.

The Lord saw it was not good for man to be alone. It would seem as if God is all we need, but Genesis tells us because God made us in the image of himself, we are created for relationship. Thus, even in the Garden of Eden, Adam was lonely until God gave him Eve. So when Adam saw Eve, he sprang into song: "bone from my bone, and flesh from my flesh" (Genesis 2:23). This is not just an ode to man and woman. It is also an ode to friendship.

GENESIS TELLS US THAT BECAUSE GOD MADE US IN THE IMAGE OF HIMSELF, WE ARE CREATED FOR RELATIONSHIP.

FROM CONVERSATION TO FRIENDSHIP

My family moved from Chesapeake, Virginia, to Richmond, Virginia, the summer before I started high school. I remember the fear of watching my old driveway fade in the distance. I lived next door to my best friend, and now that was over.

High school in a new city began with the terrible anxieties of loneliness and fear that plague all of us when we don't have a friend who walks beside us.

For that reason, I can still remember the moment in tenth grade when I met my then (and now) best friend, Steve. It was exactly how C. S. Lewis describes the moment that friendships are born—"when one person says to another: 'What! You too? I thought I was the only one.'"[1]

We both skateboarded. We both played the drums. We both projected a false confidence to hide our deep insecurities. We both desperately wanted to be popular. And we both went to the same youth group. In the best and worst of things, we found a seed of friendship in the mutual exclamation, "You too?!"

But seeds of friendship must be watered through conversation. I remember sitting by campfires and talking late into the night. I remember road trips where we talked a lot. I remember lying on floors in sleeping bags, talking after everyone else had fallen asleep. The reason Steve and I became inseparably close was because, beyond shared activities, we shared words.

Without the work of real conversation, where your deepest hopes are admitted and your greatest secrets are revealed, relationships remain based merely on common interests.

Vulnerability and time turn people who have a relationship into people who have a friendship. That's what friendship is: vulnerability across time. The practice of conversation is the basis of friendship because it's in conversation that we become exposed to each other.

This is not to dismiss the importance of shared identities, shared activities, shared concerns, and all the other things that spark friendship. This is only to say that it's through conversation that we disclose our loves for such things and, by doing so, disclose our very selves.

In her book *Reclaiming Conversation*, Sherry Turkle says that conversation "exposes" us, revealing our vulnerability, in two ways.[2]

The first way that we are exposed is in the regular risk of face-to-face, in-person conversation. Turkle explains that we're less predictable and less guarded in a conversation compared to the planning and intent to how we text or post.

When eye contact, tone of voice, and our natural responses are replaced with planned and edited replies, conversation disappears and genuine friendship is jeopardized.[3]

For many high schoolers, face-to-face time has been replaced by Facetime. In a 2022 study, only 32 percent of high school seniors said they gathered with friends in person almost every day. That's down from 44 percent in 2010.[4] Instead of talking, many teens say they prefer texting. That sends a message but not always the right one.

Turkle interviewed college students who felt "unrehearsed real-time conversation is something that makes you 'unnecessarily' vulnerable."[5] But to be vulnerable is precisely the point of conversation, because in vulnerability we are finally truly known.

The second way conversation exposes us is by the truth telling that happens in it. This goes beyond the risk of being face-to-face and further into the risk of the question my friend and I asked in the living room that night: *Is there anything you aren't telling me?* There's nothing more terrifying and redemptive than removing the mask and telling who you are to a friend.

Friendships embody the power of the gospel in a unique way, because in friendship we live out the truth of the gospel to each other. What is the gospel besides the truth that Jesus knows how broken we are and sticks around to love us anyway? What is a friend except someone who knows how broken we are, yet sticks around to love us anyway?

Conversation is the place we become truly known. Looking back to the year when Steve and I became friends, I see the real blossom of friendship between him and me. It wasn't in common interests but in common conversation. It was when we began to tell each other the things we wouldn't tell anyone else: what we wanted to do with our lives, who we wanted to become, who we liked, and what we were scared of.

Much of friendship comes from admitting the things that make us seem fragile when spoken out loud. This is why friendship is so hard. Vulnerability is risky, and time is limited.

CONVERSATION IS THE PLACE WE BECOME TRULY KNOWN.

We need the courage to be vulnerable in a world that is scared, and we need to make it a priority to take time in a world that is distracted. The habit of a weekly hour in conversation can cultivate both.

THE POWER OF VULNERABILITY

Let's go back to the story I mentioned at the outset of this chapter, the fall evening when my friend and I asked each other, "Is there anything you aren't telling me?"

Well, the next night, there was a knock on my door. That same friend was on the porch. When I opened the door and saw him standing silently, I knew something was wrong.

"We need to talk," he said. I'll never forget the combination of fear and courage in his eyes. "You remember the question we asked last night, about anything we haven't told each other?" he continued.

I knew where this was going. I knew it because the look in his eyes took me back ten years to when I was sitting with my dad at a restaurant. I was in college, waiting to work up the courage to tell him I had been lying to him—and lying for a long time. Telling the truth can be hard, telling someone that you haven't been telling the truth is even harder.

That's what my friend was doing. He was holding back something. He had lied the night before. Boldly and to my face. But now, with even more boldness, he had come back to tell the truth.

That conversation was hard on both of us. For him, because of the guilt he felt. For me, because of the feeling I had of being shut out of his life.

What he said will always stay between him and me. It was plenty serious, a struggle deep and dark enough that if not exposed to the light of conversation it might have overtaken him.

Unexposed lies rot our souls because lies open us up to the influences of the evil one. And lies always threaten the lifeblood of relationship.

So often I'm tempted to believe the fiction that our enemy is more like a cat that I can shoo away than a lion that is "crouching at the door," waiting to pounce on us (Genesis 4:7; see also 1 Peter 5:8). No matter how hard we try, we aren't immune to the dangerous temptations of life.

We aren't immune but we are provided help, through friendships and from God. In Hebrews 2:18, the writer reminds us that because Jesus "himself suffered when he was tempted, he is able to help those who are being tempted" (NIV).

When I was barely twenty and envisioning a future for me and my friends, I had no idea how difficult life alongside each other would be. I had no idea that before I was thirty, I would have friends look me in the eye and say, "I don't believe in this Jesus anymore." I had no idea I would have friends who would call me and give details of what happened at a nightclub the night before. I had no idea I would have friends sit me down and confess addictions to alcohol, prescription drugs, or pornography. Perhaps more importantly, I had no idea I would be calling them to confess that at the age of twenty-nine I needed pills or alcohol just to fall asleep. As my years and experiences have mounted up, I've come to grips with the startling evil in the world.

In Genesis, God told Cain that sin was crouching at his door, wanting to rule over him (Genesis 4:7). I used to think that story was about someone else. Now I see it's about all of us. I read it and I see myself, and I see the people I love most. I see the world as a place where lions prowl, desperate to tear us apart. But inevitably the most vicious lion is within. This cub is born as a little secret that *no one needs to know*, and it grows into a monster that rips us apart from the inside.

This is the truth of the darkness within. But the darkness is never as powerful as the light.

Vulnerable friendships have power: together we beat back the darkness by exposing it to light. When the darkness of our lives is exposed by the light of vulnerable conversation, the power of the gospel changes us. That night in the restaurant when I confessed to my dad, he forgave me, and my whole life turned around. That fall night on my porch after that friend came back to tell the truth, his life completely pivoted.

Do you notice the common thread in all the situations I just mentioned? All of these secrets, doubts, and addictions were *spoken*. They all were brought to light through words. And that light helped to bring about change.

That one friend believes in Jesus again. The other quit the nightclubs. The addicts are clean. And I've learned to drink responsibly, even on the evenings I can't fall asleep, which are now—praise God—almost never.

> VULNERABLE FRIENDSHIPS HAVE POWER: TOGETHER WE BEAT BACK THE DARKNESS BY EXPOSING IT TO LIGHT.

We'll never rid ourselves of the darkness of sin, but honest conversation brings light. And the incredible thing about God's light is that the light always wins.

THE POWER OF TIME

Vulnerable friendships that embody the gospel don't happen because we wish them into being. They happen because they're cultivated over time. They grow because we arrange them on the trellis of habit that allows them to flourish.

That's why cultivating habits to devote time to friendships is so important. Research shows it takes students forty-three hours of time together to go from acquaintances to causal friends. In another fifty-seven hours, those casual friends become actual friends who experience the kind of vulnerable friendship I'm talking about.[6]

Not all that time has to be in deep conversation; some will be enjoying shared interests, such as music, sports, video games, or hobbies. But the more time we spend together, the deeper our conversations can become.

The usual life in America leans toward busying ourselves with things that feel urgent but aren't. Friendships never seem urgent, yet they are.

The Common Rule habit of a weekly hour of conversation is aimed directly at this struggle. The idea is to cultivate a keystone habit of being the vulnerable, relational person you were created to be. That includes when life becomes complicated, because those are the times when friends are precisely what we need most.

You can cultivate weekly touch points for conversation in all kinds of ways. Standing coffee get-togethers. Grabbing breakfast or brunch on the weekend. A community group, or even a board game night. There are as many ways to do this as there are conversations to have.

The point is that weekly touch points of open conversation sustain the lifeblood of our friendships across time. Without them, we would be people who used to have friends. With them, we are friends.

OPEN CIRCLE OF FRIENDSHIP

It was my junior year of high school. Steve and I were just about to jump into a friend's convertible to drive downtown. Suddenly, someone else showed up and asked to join. He was a freshman. We didn't know him well, but we couldn't think of a good reason to say no.

During the drive it became clear he had good taste in music and an even better sense of humor. But for most of the ride, we weren't quite sure how he'd made his way into our car. We didn't even know his name.

Regardless, it was clear he wanted a friend. But Steve and I weren't willing to open up.

Like friendship, food, work, and everything else that God made, the better something is, the more it can be twisted. One of the darkest twists on friendship is our tendency to ruin it by making it exclusive.

As most of us have experienced, there are few deeper pains than the feeling of being shut out of friendship. Sadly, that's what Steve and I did. We saw our friendship as something to protect, not something to share.

I remember this season being painful for everyone. For this new guy, because he was looking for a friend and we initially denied him. It was painful for Steve and me because any blessing you try to hoard for yourself begins to sour. We ruin the goodness of blessings when we refuse to use them to bless others.

Keeping friendships closed is a broken twist on what true friendship is. The fundamental truth of friendships is not that love is limited but that love is *infinite*.

We know this because the friendship of the Trinity did not generate less love but more love. By virtue of making humans like him, God in creation expanded his circle of friends. Jesus now calls us his friends (see John 15:15), and by saving us he invites us into the communion of the Trinity. The circle of love is open and expanding.

The nature of true friendships is not to shut the outsider out, it is to draw them in.

Despite our initial selfish intention to keep this new person at arm's length, Steve and I continued to spend time and share conversation with him. Soon we began to see the fire burned bigger and brighter for all of us with him in the circle. We had new moments of saying, “You too?”

As our life of common interests turned into a life of common conversations, this new friend got to see all the good and all the bad in us. This is, of course, the truth of looking closely into anyone’s life, followers of Jesus included. Most particularly, he saw the ways we did and did not live up to the faith we claimed to have. This is not a shiny story: on the way to all becoming the best of friends, we hurt each other a lot. We made big mistakes.

This new friend saw all of this. And after seeing it, he looked beyond us to the Jesus that we worshiped. Not only did he *look* at Jesus, this friend believed in Jesus as Savior and was baptized. His name is Matt.

Matt’s friendship is a continual reminder that the fire of friendship is contagious. Opening outward is the truest direction of friendship. The circle grows. In friendship, one plus one equals three or even four. The circle is complete, but it is somehow still open. Love defies mathematics and geometry.

If friendship is a practice that reminds us of what the gospel is, it is also a practice that puts the gospel on display to the world. In a culture of loneliness and individualism, there is no better witness than embodying a counterculture of real friendship.

Friendships light up the darkness. For that reason, think of friendships as little fires we tend. They light up the truth of the gospel, they invite people into the warmth, and they become the fires around which many can gather.

To cultivate the practice of a weekly hour of conversation is to keep the fire burning. It is to look out into a cold and dark world and to offer some light, some warmth, and a place to sit and talk.

THINK ABOUT IT . . .

1. Is there anyone in your life right now who knows everything about you? Even your deepest secrets? Do you wish there were someone? You don't have to tell everyone everything, but consider telling someone everything.

2. A key claim of this chapter is that the gospel is reflected when someone knows you fully and loves you anyway. Do you agree? Why or why not?

3. Many find getting together with friends easy but getting to vulnerable conversation hard. Steve and I grew closer by talking about what we wanted to do with our lives, who we wanted to become, who we liked, and what we were scared of. Brainstorm some questions that might help you move toward more intentional and honest conversation.

4. Friendship can be a tough habit to discuss, because we cannot create a friendship alone. Many of us wish for someone who loves us well and who we can share our secrets with. If you don't have that one (or two) vulnerable friendships, take some time to pray on this. If you do, thank God for those friends.

WEEKLY HABIT 1

ONE HOUR OF CONVERSATION WITH A FRIEND

THE HABIT AT A GLANCE

We were made for each other. We can't become lovers of God and neighbor without vulnerable friendships that are sustained across time. During habitual, face-to-face conversation with each other, we find a gospel practice. We open up to each other, share our deepest desires and secrets, and are loved anyway.

THREE WAYS TO START

Standing meeting. Try setting up a standing time with a friend—such as every Thursday evening or every Saturday afternoon—when you always get together. Don't be discouraged by the fact that you have to miss every once in a while. Be encouraged by the fact that the rule is getting together to talk, and the exception is sometimes missing it.

For teammates. There are all kinds of "teams" you can be part of—sports, band, drama, clubs. These groups gather to share common interests and are great places to find new friends. If you're looking for a friend, join a team. Relationships on a team form naturally. Then look for the person, or people, where conversation flows most easily and honestly.

From acquaintance to friend. Setting up a weekly time to eat, get coffee, or just talk can be the keystone habit that moves you from just acquaintances to real friends. Consider setting up a time and coming up with questions that go beyond the shallow details of life to deeper issues. Maybe even turn off your phones so you can talk about life without other distractions.

THREE CONSIDERATIONS

On telling secrets. The question is not how to tell secrets; everyone knows how. The question is whether it's worth it or not. With someone you trust and who loves you, it always is. Tell your secrets. Do it tonight. It will change your life and will probably inspire your friends to tell theirs too. There's no better catalyst for deep relationships than telling your secrets.

The power of good questions. Often great conversations come from someone who has mastered the art of good questions. If that isn't you, consider brainstorming with your friends to come up with some good questions you can regularly ask each other.

Open friendships. While the goal of weekly conversation is to create closeness, it ends in openness. Gospel friendships don't just bear fruit for two friends together; they also offer nourishment to the world. Think of your spaces of friendship as one of the first places to invite a new person you meet.

HONEST CONVERSATION BRINGS LIGHT TO THE DARKEST PLACES.

WEEKLY HABIT 2

FOUR HOURS OF PHYSICAL ACTIVITY

I hope all is well with you and that you are as healthy in body as you are strong in spirit.

THE APOSTLE JOHN IN A LETTER TO THE EARLY CHURCH (3 JOHN 1:2)

I was never the star quarterback in high school. And you won't find any of my monster dunks plastered on YouTube (that's because there weren't any).

But I wasn't a couch potato either. Early on I played the cymbals in the drumline. Then I went to the bass drum, the snare drum, and ultimately the four tenor drums that we called *quads*.

If you've ever thought band is for students who aren't athletic, think again. Physically, drumline was as challenging as most sports. We'd be out marching on the field early in the morning and late into the night.

Practices were grueling. Blisters. Bleeding hands. Tape on the fingers. I suffered through it all. And did I mention the deep marks and bruises on my shoulders from the harness that hooked thirty- to forty-five-pound drums to me?

Imagine marching around a football field in perfect timing, while keeping an exact beat on a drum. Your hands ache. Your back feels like it's going to give out. You perform as best you can. Then the instructor says, "It's not right, do it again."

You do it again. But again, you hear, "It's not right. Do it again."

It doesn't sound fun.

Yet as I look back on the drumline in high school, it was a place of a lot of friendship. It was a place of a lot of discipline. We bonded as a group through this sense of disciplining ourselves together. And we knew we were doing something hard—*together*. We faced the challenge together. Somehow it was really fun, even though it wasn't comfortable.

A lot of people experience this on sports teams. There's something exciting and energizing about pushing through physical difficulty together. It's not about winning. It's about competing, failing, and enduring as a team. We know that physical activity makes people more physically healthy. But it also improves mental well-being, lowers stress, creates social connections, and teaches life skills such as goal-setting, self-control, and perseverance.[1]

The weekly habit of at least four hours of physical activity isn't meant to merely get our bodies moving. Yes, God created our bodies to run, jump, walk, dance, and play—and exercise is one way to stay healthy. But following this habit of physical activity results in understanding a deeper spiritual truth as well. One of the purposes of this habit is to help us explore the significant ways that we can invite God to discipline our souls as we work to discipline our bodies.

THE BODY TEACHES THE SOUL

The Bible teaches us that the body and soul are not separate, but deeply related. How we treat one affects the other.

When we exercise our bodies, we are developing more than just our muscles. When we practice discipline and do hard things, whether we "feel like it" or not, we are building up our spirit, our soul.

The apostle Paul often uses sports metaphors in his letters to the early churches, telling Christ followers to "discipline" their bodies, run with purpose, and race to win (see 1 Corinthians 9:24-27). When Paul talks about the body, he often talks about mastering the body in order to master the soul.

Earlier in his letter to the church in Corinth, Paul says this: "Don't you realize that your body is the temple of the Holy Spirit, who lives in you and was given to you by God? You do not belong to yourself, for God bought you with a high price. So you must honor God with your body" (1 Corinthians 6:19-20).

Specifically, Paul was talking about sexual sin in these verses. But his words also speak volumes about the importance of our bodies.

God made us with bodies. He redeemed us through a body. He's going to resurrect us to a body. He must care a lot about bodies!

Pause a moment and think about the implications of that truth.

We don't want to de-emphasize the spirituality of caring for our bodies, but we also don't want to overdo concern for our bodies at the expense of the spiritual disciplines.

Because the fact is, physical disciplines should lead to spiritual disciplines, and vice versa.

TEAMWORK MAKES THE DREAM WORK

We cannot do much of anything on our own. Really. For anything hard—and most of life is hard—we need other people to help us persevere. No one perseveres alone. It is together that we push forward. This is why communal routines—whether attending church, practicing a sport, or going to an exercise class—are so effective.

When I exercise alone, I have a much lower threshold of where I'm likely to say, "I'm done. I'm not finishing the workout. It's too hard."

But when I'm around my friends, or other people in an exercise class, there's this mutual sense that we can finish it together. If I'm tired, the instructor or a friend can encourage me to keep going. And if I see a teammate struggling, I'm able to encourage them to make it to the end.

Whether physical activities or spiritual disciplines, we realize that we possess way more capacity than we thought when we do it together.

I tell my kids all the time: "We do hard things." I tell them this because hard things can help us learn. It's often our greatest challenges and the events that present our deepest struggles that promote the most growth in our lives. It's an odd truth, but a central and biblical one that God shows us repeatedly in the Scriptures.

> ALMOST ANYTHING THAT CREATES GROWTH IN OUR LIVES HURTS AT THE TIME.

Pain and hardship are unavoidable in life; they are not something to be feared but actually embraced as sanctifying forces. Don't get me wrong. This is not *stoicism*—mentally trying to not let pain affect you. Neither is this *masochism*, as if pain is actually pleasure. Though exercise is not the suffering of undeserved deep affliction or loss, it *is* hard work and through it we can learn self-control and the discipline of perseverance in the face of adversity (see Romans 5:3-5; 1 Corinthians 9:24-27).

The body teaches the soul. To internalize this discipline, it's good for us to subject ourselves to healthy activity daily.

Experts say teens need about an hour of moderate- to high-intensity exercise every day. But only one in four teens achieves this standard. The minimum recommendation is thirty minutes of exercise, three times a week.[2] This habit of at least four hours of physical activity each week can be an hour a day for four days, or split up any way that best fits your schedule.

Before you get started, be sure to talk to a parent or guardian as well as your doctor if you have any health conditions. But typically, an easy place to start is by walking with family or friends. Eventually, look for ways to increase the difficulty level while doing something you enjoy. Join a climbing gym. Go out for a sport. Play pickleball. Perform with a drumline. Attend a spin class with friends.

Whatever your preferred physical activity, "Just do it."

By choosing to voluntarily do challenging physical activities, we embrace the idea that life isn't easy. There's hardship and difficulty. And in any challenge, we can connect with and rely on Christ.

THE END IS THE BEGINNING

At times in our lives we may think, "I'm done. I can't do that." We can feel frustrated by our parents or out of patience with our siblings or friends. Other times it may be a habit we can't kick or a sin that gets us stuck.

"I just can't do it," you may say.

And you may be right. But this is the point where Jesus will come in and say, "When you think you're at your end, I'm coming in to call you past it. Because at the end of yourself, there is more of me."

Finding the end of yourself is finding the beginning of God's grace. Those were the Lord's words to Paul in 2 Corinthians 12:9: "My grace is all you need. My power works best in weakness."

As a father and a lawyer, I often reach a point where I feel like I don't have any more patience to deal with children, or I don't have any more time to deal with the stress of clients. Yet both of these positions require me to continue to work even when I have nothing left. And this teaches me something. When I think there is nothing left, there is actually something left: it is God's grace. And his grace is sufficient. It carries me through difficult times.

Paul reminds us that it's in our weakness that we find God's grace. Exercise is a terrific practice field to experience this. During most workouts, there's often a point where we say, "I don't want to go on. In fact, I can't go on."

But something happens when we reach that point and decide to go on anyway: we realize the wall is not the wall. There is more of ourselves beyond ourselves, and that is what I call the "space of grace."

In this space, we can't or could not have done it on our own. But suddenly, we're able to do more than we ever thought we could do.

That is God's grace. It strengthens us when we have no strength left.

Sometimes this grace is in our failure. We don't win. We don't achieve a personal record. We don't complete our workout goal. It's okay. It's okay to reach your end. It's also okay to keep trying even after you've failed and met your end. Because when we persevere, we meet the grace we were made for.

The Bible is unashamed about tying hardship to character. In so many other worldviews, suffering is to be avoided at all costs. But in the biblical story, God redeems suffering and creates meaning through it instead.

Through physical training, we experience this paradigm of hardship producing growth. By doing difficult things, becoming uncomfortable, letting our bodies suffer physically, we grow—in body, in mind, in heart.

When we cling to God in our challenges—whether in exercise or undeserved suffering—he uses it to soften our hearts and firm our character. But when we avoid finding God in our hardships, we end up with hardened hearts and weakened characters. So it is not the act of suffering itself that we look to for hope, but God's grace in using hardship that produces character and ultimately hope (see Romans 5:3-5).

WHEN WE CLING TO GOD IN OUR CHALLENGES, HE USES IT TO SOFTEN OUR HEARTS AND FIRM OUR CHARACTER.

Consider holding this thought in your mind during your next workout or practice.

You do not have to fear doing hard things; you do not have to avoid it—you can walk bravely into it, knowing that God will use it to create hope.

KNOW THE GOAL

Hope changes everything. The power of hope is that we draw strength in the present by envisioning our future. This happens during exercise all the time.

It is often the hope of making the team, making a time, or simply feeling better and being healthy that motivates us to work out today.

But consider this: no single workout changes us in any way that we can tell. It is always a stretch of time and consistent workouts that slowly lead to a better future. This takes endurance and patience. And hope is what keeps us going.

All the best things in life take perseverance over the long haul. In 1 Corinthians 9:24-25, Paul teaches us that to be a Christian over the course of our lives is like running a race. We have to train, work, endure, expect difficulty, and try with all our might to prevail. This is a spirit of endurance (remember Romans 5).

To complete our homework and earn good grades is hard. To obey our parents is hard. To be a faithful friend is hard. To stick with going to church despite busy schedules and conflict with others is hard. But when we endure in these areas, we see the benefits of closer relationships and a brighter future.

Jesus called us to go further and empowered us with the Holy Spirit to carry us through any difficult time. And by practicing this habit of physical activity with friends, we develop an additional support system.

Recently, one of my friends ran a marathon. Before the race, he asked several friends to stand at the last five miles. His plan was to have a person at each mile near the end of the race to encourage him. He wanted us to pace him by riding a bike next to him and say, "You got this. Keep going."

The friends who helped him said he was mad during those final miles. Instead of smiling when he saw someone waiting for him, he got angry. He was at the end of himself and wanted to slow down. But he didn't—he kept on going because someone was there, encouraging him to finish.

The result?

He set a personal record. In fact, his time was so fast that he qualified to run the Boston Marathon!

When he crossed the finish line, all his anger was gone. Instead he was filled with joy and gratefulness. He'd run faster than he'd ever run before, and he knew it was because of his friends' encouraging actions and words—"Go! You got this!"

God does the same for us but to an even greater degree. We were once at the end of ourselves, truly dead. That's when Jesus showed up and said, "You can run a better race. You can live an abundant life."

When we listen and follow him, we find a part of us that comes alive as we realize there's more of us at the end of us. That's the space of grace.

THINK ABOUT IT . . .

1. How would you describe your current level of activity? (Select one.)

   ○ Sloth: I barely move.
   ○ Dog: I'm active with my friends.
   ○ Hummingbird: I'm always on the go.

2. Have you ever accomplished something difficult with a group of people? What happened? How did the experience bond you together?

3. How might being physically disciplined lead to being spiritually disciplined?

4. How can we discover a deeper meaning of God's grace through physical activity?

WEEKLY HABIT 2

FOUR HOURS OF PHYSICAL ACTIVITY

THE HABIT AT A GLANCE

God created our bodies to move. Physical activity not only strengthens muscles and bones, but also builds up our spirit and soul. Through intense physical activity, we can discover that at the end of ourselves there is a lot more of God. And in this space of grace, we find that in hardship—especially shared with a team or friend—we build character and find hope.

THREE WAYS TO START

Get on your marks. Like every habit, starting an exercise routine takes planning and determination. Before you begin, make sure you talk with your parent or guardian and your doctor if you have any health conditions. And then dedicate yourself to doing something active every day for five days. If you don't have a favorite physical activity, try a variety of them. Swim. Bike. Walk. Try pickleball. There's no one-size-fits-all workout. Keep trying different activities until you find something you want to make a habit.

Get set. Don't do this alone, especially if you're not a naturally active person. No change happens outside of accountability. By inviting someone to join you, you'll get stronger together. Plus, you'll have that voice encouraging you to do one more push-up or run one more block.

Go . . . and then stop. I'm not a patient person. When I start something, I want to see results right away. So if I'm exercising,

I might overdo it in an effort to experience change right away. That can be a recipe for disaster. Anyone who knows anything about physical training will tell you it's not the exercise that makes you stronger. It's the rest and recovery after exercise that allow your muscles to repair and grow. Without rest, you won't get stronger.

THREE CONSIDERATIONS

How we treat our bodies is a spiritual matter. Our bodies are a physical representation of Christ. We are image-bearers of God. What we eat matters. How much sleep we get matters. Our level of activity matters. How we care for our bodies—our habits of diet, rest, and exercise—honor God as our Creator and Savior.

Exercise your brain. Walking has been shown to create connections between brain cells, promote better memory, and inspire creativity. Some of my deepest thoughts and best prayers come as I walk. And as I mentioned at the beginning of this book, it was a walk that prompted me to change my path in life and become a lawyer. So get moving and see how your thoughts, and life, might change.

Make it work for you. Maybe you're suffering from an injury or an illness that makes exercise difficult for you right now. Don't sweat it, literally. Do what you can. Whether it's fitness bands in a chair or light stretching, find a level of physical activity that will lead you to a healthier lifestyle.

WEEKLY HABIT 3

FAST FROM SOMETHING FOR TWENTY-FOUR HOURS

When you fast, don't make it obvious.
JESUS (MATTHEW 6:16)

Dan stood out in a crowd.

Not only was he good-looking, he checked all the boxes.

Athletic. *Check.*
Smart. *Double check.*
Well-mannered. *Triple check.*

Normally, standing out in a crowd was a good thing for Dan. But when a mighty kingdom invaded Dan's country, standing out meant being taken away.

The conquering king didn't just claim gold and jewels. He took the best and brightest young men and made them march nine hundred miles to his palace. The king wanted to train these teenagers to serve him in his palace.

Dan was one of the first to go, so were his friends Hank, Mike, and Zari.

As soon as they entered the king's palace, they were given instructions of what they were expected to do.

"You'll read *our* most important books," the king's chief of staff told them. "You'll learn *our* language. And you'll eat only *our* foods and drink *our* wine, just like the king."

Many of the guys were excited to eat and drink so well—to feast! Not Dan and his friends. They followed strict rules about what they ate.

"Uh, Mr. Chief," Dan said. "As great as that buffet sounds, my friends and I would prefer to just eat vegetables and drink water."

"Do you want to get me killed?" the chief of staff exclaimed. "If you get all pale and weak from your veggie diet, you'll stand out from the guys who are eating the fine foods. I can't let that happen."

"Can we just try for ten days?" Dan asked. "Let us eat the way our God has called us to. Then see what we look like."

Reluctantly, the chief of staff agreed.

Dan and his friends passed up the buffet and instead ate their veggies. And at the end of ten days, "Daniel and his three friends looked healthier and better nourished than the young men who had been eating the food assigned by the king" (Daniel 1:15).

FAST FACTS

The story of Daniel, Hananiah, Mishael, and Azariah—better known as Shadrach, Meshach, and Abednego—contains many truths. One is about the power and importance of fasting.

Fasting is mentioned over and over again in the Bible. Moses fasted before he received the Ten Commandments from God. God's prophets fasted before confronting evil rulers. King David fasted when his child was ill. Jesus fasted before starting his public ministry. The apostle Paul fasted after he encountered the risen Jesus on the road to Damascus. And Daniel and his friends fasted when they found themselves trapped in a foreign land.

The idea of a *fast* is to voluntarily give up something for a spiritual purpose. The most common type of fast is going without food. Jesus and Moses fasted from eating food for forty days. That's a *loong* time. Many Christians do it for twenty-four hours, which is what I typically recommend for adults. Before we go any further, we need to recognize that the purpose of this kind of spiritual fast isn't to lose weight. This means that if you have even the slightest issue with an eating disorder, I want you to fast from something other than food. Also, teens need proper nutrition while their bodies are growing. So if you choose to fast from food, I've got one requirement and one suggestion.

The requirement is that you can't begin fasting from food until you have discussed it with your parent or guardian and doctor first.

And then here's my suggestion: Don't go it alone. Whether your fast is with a friend, your family, or your entire youth group, like just about anything in life, it is better when it's done together.

But you don't have to fast from food! *Anything* that makes us feel a longing can be given up for a fast. We can go without playing video games, eating chocolate, looking at our phone, consuming energy drinks. If it's part of our daily routine and important to us, it can be given up as a fast.

Go back and look at the definition of a fast. You *voluntarily* give up something for a *spiritual* purpose.

But if going without food only makes me "hangry," then I've missed the point. A fast should make us long—and even *hunger*—for God. Whether it's through prayer, Bible reading, or quiet mediation, we fill ourselves with godly pursuits during the time we'd normally give to the activity or item we're giving up.

For this reason we need to be intentional about what we go without in order for our fasts to be healthy. Daniel and his friends fasted from *certain* foods, not *all* food, when they were teens.

The point of fasting is not the technicalities and rigidity of it. The point is to *lean into the lack*. We should hunger, and long, and ache for what we're willingly going without. This can be done in many, many ways.

Whatever fast you choose to do, it may appear as a radical act, especially to your friends. Here in the United States, fasting is bizarrely countercultural because it runs the opposite direction of the American dream. In pursuit of this dream, we strive to move upward in the world through sheer individual effort. Ultimately, the belief is we'll finally be happy when we get the most and the best. In fasting, we deliberately move toward emptiness—and even more, we admit that we can't eat or work or play our way to happiness. We need God for that.

FASTING AND FEASTING

When God made Adam and Eve, he set them in the Garden of Eden, where the trees were beautiful and produced delicious fruit (Genesis 2:9). God's people had no needs. They had an abundance of food because God is generous. He makes wonderful things. When we feast with grateful hearts, we celebrate God's gift of food. In fact, when we enjoy any of the gifts God has given us, we celebrate his goodness and generosity.

After Adam and Eve chose to eat the fruit from the forbidden tree, they inverted God's gift. They ate to *become* God instead of to *celebrate* God. The fall changed everything.

Fasting is a way to resist the sin of seeking happiness solely in earthly things and instead to look to God for our joy. So instead of eating our way to happiness, we look to God for our fullness. In that sense, to fast is to lean into a key truth: we are empty without God. As it says in Deuteronomy 8:3, "People do not live by bread alone; rather, we live by every word that comes from the mouth of the LORD."

TO FAST IS TO LEAN INTO A KEY TRUTH: WE ARE EMPTY WITHOUT GOD.

In the Bible, fasting doesn't just reveal and clarify our own need for God. It encourages us to lean into the suffering of the world itself and to long for God to redeem it.

This is why the Israelites fasted during the time of Esther; they knew the brokenness and injustice of the leaders they lived under, and they longed for God to save them.

This is partly why Jesus fasted before he began his ministry. He was sent to rescue us from the fall. His fast was an act of longing for the world to be restored by his ministry to come.

The weekly habit of fasting, then, is a way to lean into both the emptiness of the world as it is and prayer for the coming fullness of the world as it will be. The world doesn't end in fasting, of course, but in a feast the Bible calls "the wedding feast of the Lamb" (see Revelation 19:6-9).

FASTING REVEALS OUR INNER EMPTINESS

It's almost silly to talk about the American view of comfort because, well, it's obviously extravagant. We like to indulge, on nearly everything. Americans seem to always want more.

But fasting from anything exposes this. It exposes our inner emptiness because when we fast we can't use things—food, phones, caffeine, busyness—to dull our desires, numb our feelings, or make us feel satisfied or happy.

My emptiness is the first thing I notice when I fast from food. No matter how regularly I do it, it always hits me like a surprise. "Oh no! I can't eat today."

Almost immediately I feel depressed. Normally, I don't realize how breakfast sets my emotional tone for the day. But during a fast, when I don't have breakfast, I honestly feel myself sinking into despair, and hunger hasn't even started yet.

It's midmorning when I become irritable. Not only am I trying to concentrate over a growling stomach, but I also can't do what I otherwise do every day: look forward to lunch or snacks as a way to distract myself from work.

Then I move from irritation to anger, and impatience leaks out of me everywhere.

That's not a pretty picture. But that's sort of the point of the practice of fasting: seeing who we really are.

When I fast, I see that deep down I'm not actually a very patient person. I'm not actually a very content person. I'm not as independent and strong as I thought I was. I'm a weak, impatient, angry person who medicates with food and drink. This is painful to confront. Yet to live without fasting is to live without knowing who I truly am.

Fortunately, this is not the end point of the fasting experience. For when we give up "bread," we can then fill ourselves with the second part of the verse from Deuteronomy—"every word that comes from the mouth of the LORD."

When I fast, I try to set aside the time that I would be eating to spend time in prayer. By praying, I'm filled in a way that, although my stomach is empty, my soul is satisfied.

Fasting is designed to let our desires hang out in the open, where we can observe them in a clarity that is impossible without the act of fasting. I see more who I really am, and I feel more of who God really is. Slowly but surely, my posture in relation to the world is recalibrated. I'm not here to get what I want; I'm here to love other people.

I come home in the evenings on those days not expecting to eat. I simply expect to serve other people as they eat. The most remarkable part is that I'm actually happier, because instead of believing that food makes me happy, I recognize that only love does that.

FASTING REVEALS THE WORLD'S NEED

Still, the happiness doesn't take away the longing. During those evenings I will listen to music or a podcast or take a walk and pray as a distraction. On a particular night several years ago, I did both.

At the time I was living in a neighborhood on the north side of downtown Richmond called Jackson Ward that was close to my law firm. As I walked that evening, I realized every time I left my door I walked south. I did that because that's where my office was. That's where the library, YMCA, good coffee shops, and bakeries were.

In short, my life was south of my house. But that night I walked north. I'd just finished listening to Dr. Martin Luther King's address at Stanford University from 1967. In it, he described two Americas. "Every city in our country has this kind of dualism," he said, "this schizophrenia, split at so many parts, and so every city ends up being two cities rather than one. There are two Americas."[1]

That night, I knew what he was talking about. Just north of my house was Gilpin Court, the largest public housing project in Richmond. It was closer to my house than my office. I walked to my office every day, but I had never walked to Gilpin Court. Not once. The life expectancy in Gilpin Court was twenty years less than in my neighborhood. Roughly one of every three males born in Gilpin Court went to jail.

How these "two Americas" developed in Richmond is terribly complicated, but the reality of living in the area was terribly obvious. The city was busted up. One side of the bridge that went over the interstate felt safe. The other side felt dangerous.

On that night, as I walked two blocks north and stood at the bridge, I could see into the other America. A man in a hoodie passed me. I watched his movements carefully; he watched mine. Neither of us could see each other's eyes. Across the bridge were vacant lots without trees. A blinking sign advertised malt liquor at the only open store. Around the corner I saw a flashing blue light and heard police sirens.

Dr. King had given his "The Other America" speech more than fifty years beforehand, calling attention to the radically different lives and opportunities Americans have. Yet looking around, I couldn't see much had changed. Those two Americas still existed.

Overwhelmed by the weight of it all, I sat down on a bench and began to pray.

"Lord," I remember saying, "tell me what to do. I know you know, and you can tell me. Just tell me what I can do about this. Right now, please speak."

Then I waited. I sat in stillness, leaning forward. "I will tell everyone," I prompted, "just tell me now what we can do."

Suddenly, I sensed light all around me. When I looked up, I saw red, white, and blue lights. An ambulance and a police car whipped around the corner, sirens blaring. I could feel the rumble of their engines. They accelerated past me, lights spinning into the night of Gilpin Court. Then I lost sight of them, and all was quiet. I sat on the bench waiting for an answer, but heard only silence.

That's it? I thought. I stayed quiet for another long, sad period of time. Then I walked home.

It's clear to me now why God answered me with silence that night. Silence is the hallmark of vulnerable individuals. They are vulnerable for many reasons, but this may be the main one: When they call, no one answers.

It's not because they can't talk, not because they don't have something important to say. It's because the system drowns them out. The tapestry of justice is torn in just the right way to obscure their voices.

We could talk about how everyone is vulnerable in their own ways. And it would be true. But the fact is that it doesn't have to be this way.

It's the way it is *because* we have made it that way.

When we fast, we become more attuned to the reality of the world's suffering. Many of our neighbors' sufferings are out in the open; they need to be seen. Confronted. Named. Especially by those, like me, who do not suffer as they do.

Even when we don't know what to do or how, it's important simply to cut through the silence. That's a step toward loving justice. So while there is a part of fasting that reveals our own need, there is a part that reveals the world's need too.

To fast is to lean into the emptiness that seems to run under all of us and simply say, "Yes, it's there, and it's there for my neighbors too." This kind of fasting is a way to lean past our own emptiness and into someone else's. It's a practice of empathy, of willingly walking into pain for someone else.

WHEN WE FAST, WE BECOME MORE ATTUNED TO THE REALITY OF THE WORLD'S SUFFERING.

FASTING REVEALS THE ONE WHO MEETS ALL NEEDS

As I look back at the evening I walked to the edge of Gilpin Court, nothing has changed. Not that I can see. Yes, I have been changed. But there is still so much more I want to see redeemed in this corner of Richmond. Yet these problems of poverty and vulnerability seem as immovable as the James River that runs through my city.

The reality of this side of fasting is that many of our deepest prayers aren't answered with the miracles we long for. The poverty of my neighbors lingers.

But even when our prayers aren't answered in the space that fasting opens up, we find something else: Christ. He is the one who can and will fix all of this. And he's the one we are to be with while we make an effort to do the same.

In fasting, we practice becoming like Christ, who gave himself up. Fasting is a way to enter into Jesus' life. He was homeless and hungry. He was an outcast. He was actually—not just metaphorically—poor. He lived among violence. He died violently.

To follow Jesus is not just to believe in his life; it is also to follow him into his lifestyle. And that idea runs hard against my usual expectations of being American. It's hard to be poor in a land of opportunity. It's hard to be hungry in a land of plenty. And it's hard to be empathetic in a land where we hide the poor on the other side of the interstate. It's hard.

But fasting is a habit of breaking that comfort in order to seek true comfort. We continue to fast because that's where we find Jesus—right on the fault line of the beautiful and the broken. The miracles we see in fasting are amazing.

The prophet Daniel saw this over and over again in his life. By following God's rules and fasting as a teenager, he was lifted up to a position of prominence in Babylon. Daniel continued to follow God later in life, refusing to pray to King Darius and instead following his practice of kneeling prayer to God three times a day (see Daniel 6:10). By disobeying this law, Daniel was thrown into the lions' den. This time the king fasted for Daniel. Darius knew he'd been tricked and wanted his friend to be safe, and God saved Daniel (Daniel 6:18-22).

Daniel also fasted and prayed to God on behalf of the people of Israel on several occasions (see Daniel 9:3 and 10:2-3). God answered Daniel's prayers both times by giving him a vision of the future. God then sent the angel Gabriel to explain the vision to Daniel (Daniel 9:21-22). Some Bible scholars even believe Jesus appeared to Daniel in chapter 10. That's amazing!

But the brokenness we enter into as we fast can be unbearable. This is, I suppose, why the practice of fasting is a beautiful and painful reminder of a good world cracked by the fall.

Cultivating the habit of fasting as a way of life means cultivating an understanding of why beauty and brokenness intertwine in the present world. I know of no other way of life that can both acknowledge all that the Lord has done and still yearn for all that we desperately long for him to do.

THINK ABOUT IT . . .

1. Have you ever fasted before? What did you fast from and what did you learn?

2. What scares you about fasting or hinders you from making it a regular practice?

3. Jesus begins his teaching on fasting with this: "When you fast . . ." (Matthew 6:16). Why do you think Jesus assumed that people fasted?

4. How does fasting open us up to experience the pain of others and empathize with their suffering? Is it possible to experience deeper happiness by giving up something we enjoy? How?

5. What are some ways of fasting you think God could use in your life?

WEEKLY HABIT 3

FAST FROM SOMETHING FOR TWENTY-FOUR HOURS

THE HABIT AT A GLANCE

We constantly seek to fill our emptiness with comforts and we ignore our soul and our neighbor's need by medicating ourselves with food, drink, and other distractions. Regular fasting exposes who we really are, reminds us how broken the world is, and draws our eyes to how Jesus redeems all things.

THREE WAYS TO START

Pick something to fast from. The first step is choosing something that's helpful to fast from. For regular fasting, I prefer fasting from all food. But fasting from sugar, meat, caffeine, social media, TV, internet, video games, or something else may be a good way for you to begin regular fasting. If you choose to fast from food, be sure to talk to a parent or guardian and your doctor.

Sundown to sundown. My preferred fast begins at sundown on a Thursday and ends with a communal breaking of the fast at sundown on Friday. This is a great way to do a twenty-four hour communal fast with friends.

Start with a meal. If fasting from food intimidates you, start by skipping a meal—maybe lunch—and replacing it with prayer. If you do it with family, skip your family meal so you can pray together. If you do it with friends at school, choose lunch. Being in this rhythm with someone else makes it easier to try fasting, and the communal nature of it changes the experience.

THREE CONSIDERATIONS

Communal fasting. I find fasting far richer in community—not to mention it's hard for me to muster the discipline when I'm the only one doing it. Consider having a text or email chain among people who are fasting so you can share encouragements and prayers. Also consider doing an initial prayer time together and/or breaking the fast together.

Prayer. Usually, skipping a meal doesn't lead me to pray. I find that I need to take walks to actually pray. Whatever you do, make sure you replace whatever you're fasting from with prayer.

TO LIVE WITHOUT FASTING IS TO LIVE WITHOUT KNOWING WHO YOU TRULY ARE.

Multiple days. Although I would never recommend teens fast from food for multiple days, I can recommend occasionally fasting from social media, video games, or sugar for more than one day. I've had wonderful times meeting the Lord during longer fasts. I've also had difficult times where fasting for multiple days was the way to repentance.

SABBATH REST

> *Observe the Sabbath day by keeping it holy, as the LORD your God has commanded you. You have six days each week for your ordinary work, but the seventh day is a Sabbath day of rest dedicated to the LORD your God.*
>
> THE TEN COMMANDMENTS (DEUTERONOMY 5:12-14)

I stood in a small room while a Chinese doctor mumbled and made notes on a clipboard. He wore a white lab coat.

"How much you sleep?" he asked in broken English.

I hesitated. *Should I tell him about the spreadsheet I use to track my hours of sleep each night?* I wondered. *But the point of the spreadsheet is to minimize my sleep to five hours or less. He'll think I'm crazy!*

"Probably not enough," I responded in Chinese.

"You work lot?" he asked.

I hesitated again. I was frustrated that he was speaking English. The reason I worked around the clock was that I was trying to learn Chinese, just like the great historical missionaries to China.

I had read that Matteo Ricci, the sixteenth-century Italian Jesuit missionary to China, would ask anyone at the emperor's table to recite an ancient Chinese poem. After hearing it once, he could recite it back to his listeners verbatim—except backward. Ricci was a master of memory, which gained him incredible favor and opportunity to teach about Jesus.

Legend has it that Ricci created what is called a *memory palace*—a vast castle in his mind where he made a mental map of everything he learned. When he heard something new, he pictured setting the facts in a room in his palace. If he needed to recall something, he visualized walking back in the room and picking up the knowledge.

In China—and in many other places in the world—learning the language is a way to show honor and respect. I desperately desired to be a good missionary, so I dedicated myself to learning Chinese. I tried all kinds of strange life hacks to figure out ways—in my own efforts to be like Ricci—to push my body and mind to do more.

I tried intermittent sleeping and other methods of minimizing sleep. I bought books on speed reading and attempted to train myself to read a page in a matter of seconds. I also began keeping track of my time in fifteen-minute intervals. I scheduled every morning for reading, news, writing, and study so that by the time I left for class at eight thirty, I had already done more than many do in a day. I even tried creating my own memory palace.

But it was mostly useless.

I'd doze off when I tried not to sleep. Every time I'd speed read, I came away not having the faintest idea of what the material said. Sometimes I didn't even know what book I was reading. And even though I walked my memory palace over and over, I couldn't remember the rooms, much less what was in them.

Despite the disappointment of hitting the limits of my mind and memory, there was still a real pleasure to this period in my life. Keeping track of my time was working. It was like budgeting money—once I saw where the asset was going, I started acting differently. It also helped me learn Chinese faster.

There are few deeper satisfactions than throwing yourself headlong into good work. In fact, the paradox of good work seems to be this: Anything worth doing requires bending your whole life toward it. On the other hand, nothing is worth bending your life until it breaks.

I never seem to know where that point is until *after* I break. And during this season in China, my body broke. I developed persistent lesions—areas of swelling and inflammation—that seemed to have no cause and wouldn't go away. When one developed right over my cheekbone, I decided to go to the doctor.

"Yes, I'm working a lot," I finally said.

Then I cracked. I told him about my schedule, about the sleep minimization, about the drive that was putting my body under so much stress.

He set down his clipboard. Then for the first time in our conversation, he switched to Chinese.

"Bu yao ji," he said. That's a casual way of saying, "Don't worry." He put his hand on my shoulder. "Ni xuyao xiuxi (You need to rest)," he said with a smile.

As he spoke in his own language, his personality shifted. He seemed less of a doctor and more of a grandfather—someone I could trust.

An incredible sense of relief spread over me. And I went home.

A GOD WHO RESTS

In the beginning, God created. The book of Genesis describes how he did this for six days before sitting back. On the seventh day, God stopped. He did nothing. He took sabbath because the work was finished.

Most people in the world still organize their lives around this divine seven-day rhythm. We work. Then we call it done for the weekend. There's a reason for this. We were made for this rhythm.

Focusing and *finishing* are the two great glories of work. We focus on a project, such as researching and writing a history report. We pour ourselves into it. Then we finish it, turn it in, and check it off our lists.

The rhythms of focusing and finishing seem to be built into the DNA of what it means to be human. This is exactly why treating our bodies like machines is wrong. They weren't made to work without consistent and rhythmic pause points when we finish and rest.

As I look back on my phase of life hacks, I see something sinister. The fundamental idea was that I was a computer or a machine. All I needed to do was find solutions for my pesky limitations, like the need for sleep or rest.

OUR BODIES ARE MADE TO WORK WITH CONSISTENT AND RHYTHMIC PAUSE POINTS WHEN WE FINISH AND REST.

My envy of Matteo Ricci has always been strange, so I don't blame him for my drivenness. What I loved about him was the way he seemed to be limitless. And I loved this because I don't like my limits.

I admit I'm odd. I have always been prone to eccentricities. The speed reading and the sleep tracking are things I don't usually tell people about for a reason. (Or the fact that I still keep track of my time.) But the impulse that led me to those things seems to be universal.

None of us like our limits. Like Adam and Eve in the garden, we are not content to be *like* God; we want to *be* God. The weekly habit of sabbath rest reminds us that God is God and we are not.

BUSYNESS AS A STATUS SYMBOL

While culture still arranges time around a seven-day schedule, resting on the seventh day is now conspicuously missing.

In professions like mine—and there are many—the idea of taking a day off is at best quaint and at worst scandalous. Once I was giving a talk to sixty or seventy new, young lawyers at my firm. When I told them that in order to be good lawyers for the long haul, they need to cultivate a habit of taking one day off every week, you could have heard a pin drop.

I got the sense that if I had been more like my China self and told them about new ways to life hack away sleep and work eighty-hour weeks, they would have nodded in approval while dying a little bit inside.

It's like the way I looked at Ricci. Many of us praise the acts of being inhuman as acts of being a great human. The consequences, of course, are dreadful.

That summer in China I had to get minor surgery to remove the lesion on my cheekbone. I still bear that scar.

But I'm also grateful for that failure because that's when I learned rest is a generous gift. It's made for us, for our body and our soul. When I tried to live outside limitations, my body and soul both suffered for it.

Some people aren't so lucky. They spend great chunks of their life denying the need for rest until they crash, often much more spectacularly. I see this happening in my workplace daily, but I see it happen in my church too.

As a student you may take weekends, but your days away from school are often spent furiously trying to accomplish other things: new hobbies, sports, more clubs, a side job—anything to round out and make your college application or resume appear more impressive. If you have a spare day, you might "get your life together," organize your room, or update your various profiles that you've been meaning to take care of.

Stopping and taking a nap would be a sign of weakness or poor stewardship. Sometimes we honestly feel it's immoral to rest.

During certain times in history, the upper-class showed off their status by displaying their lives of leisure. Now we show off how important we are by displaying lives of constant busyness. The more important we are, the more in demand our time is, so nobody who is anybody has time for enough sleep.

THE RESTLESS SOUL

The need for rest goes beyond our bodies. Our souls need rest too. But the rest that our souls need is not simply a nap. It's the rest that comes with realizing we don't have anything to prove. As image-bearers of God, we don't have to prove we're important. God made us that way, put us as stewards over his creation, and even had his Son die in our place to show us his love.

In God's economy, we don't have to accomplish anything in order to be known and loved by him.

This is why our culture can't accept sabbath. It does not believe work is from God and for our neighbor. Instead many believe—and we fall into the same trap—that work is *from* us and *for* us.

We pursue productivity and accomplishments to become who we want to become. Our status defines us—valedictorian, homecoming king, honor roll, first chair, 10,000-plus followers. This is the American dream. We work our way to significance. This is what we're doing when we max out our schedule; we're trying to show that we matter, that the world wants us, that the world depends on us.

IN GOD'S ECONOMY, WE DON'T HAVE TO ACCOMPLISH ANYTHING IN ORDER TO BE KNOWN AND LOVED BY HIM.

But the gospel wants to put that to rest. We don't have to work like that because God and his Son have done the work for us. God finished the work of creation. Jesus finished the work of redemption. This is why, in his final words on the cross, Jesus cries out, "It is finished!"

What is finished? The work of salvation. In his death and resurrection, Jesus did everything needed to unite us with the God who loves us. There is not a single thing to add. But there is everything to receive.

When we receive God's gift of salvation and forgiveness, we can rest in the knowledge that there's nothing left to prove. We're important because God loves us and created us and redeemed us. Then we can finally take a day off. We can finally take a nap or stare at a cloud or have coffee and a long conversation with friends.

"It is finished" is the lullaby of all things, our restless hearts and souls included.

ALL THE DOING IN NOT DOING

As I learned in China, everyone has to rest. If we don't choose to rest, then our body will make us rest—often in the form of sickness, injury, or emotional breakdown. These tend to be painful. After that year in China, Lauren and I began to practice sabbath as a matter of necessity.

One of the first things we learned was that proper sabbath-keeping is much more about *doing* than *not doing*. It's about doing restful things. Often our inclination to stop and veg out ended up being counterproductive. Some of it was exactly what we needed, especially what our bodies needed, which is downtime and the refreshment of laughter. But our souls need more than to do nothing; they need to do *restful* things. In this sense, real rest takes real work.

In China, Lauren and I found there were certain things that rejuvenated us from the week of language learning and conversations with students. An ideal sabbath looked like this: sleep in, worship, long lunch with friends, go home and rest, maybe nap, go out and explore some part of the city we hadn't been to yet or take a walk in a park, and bring a book that was pure pleasure reading.

All these things involved doing worshipful or engaging activities. Some took planning. But all were things that drew us closer to God, to each other, and to others in our lives.

The rest I needed was not only more sleep, but it was also the rest that comes in good friendships or sitting still in God's creation.

Sabbath rest, like anything else, comes with practice. And starting this practice can be terribly difficult. The first step is to pick a day. Next, communicate about your desire to take a sabbath to the people around you.

Lauren and I set aside sundown Saturday to sundown Sunday as our sabbath. Saturday afternoon is often filled with laundry, house cleaning, and all the other things we need to get done in order to create space for rest.

We often begin our sabbath by lighting a candle. Marking time matters, and this practice has been a way to say, "Okay, we're starting now."

On Sunday morning, one of my favorite things to do is get up and cook a big breakfast before church. We eat together and usually go to the latest service possible in order to preserve the unhurried character of the morning.

My wife and I like the rhythm of Saturday evening to Sunday evening sabbaths, because then both of us have time Sunday evening to get ready for the week. This could be a time where you put the finishing touches on a project or complete that last part of homework.

COME AND SABBATH

Beginning the practice of sabbath brings almost everyone to the same realization: "I can't get it all done."

Maybe it's the laundry, maybe it's a group meeting, maybe it's science club. Whatever it is, when you plan to stop working for twenty-four hours, you come to the stubborn reminder that you can't do it all.

This is the point!

Practicing sabbath is supposed to make us feel like we can't get it all done because that's reality. We can't do it all. Sabbath rest protects us from acting out the lie that we can.

I began sabbathing out of necessity; my health depended on it. Now I sabbath as a way to understand my salvation; my soul depends on it.

When I stop working, I have to admit that the world doesn't depend on me. At times it feels like the planets will fall out of orbit if I cease to write emails. Amazingly, not only do the planets faithfully hang in space but usually no one notices I'm gone!

Sabbath helps me see how small I am. When I don't see that, I'm prone to misunderstand the reality of who is dependent on who.

The belief that we sustain the world and God doesn't is at the core of our un-rest. The violence of that belief shows up as scars on the heart and the body. I still bear mine on my left cheekbone. In the deep stillness of habitual sabbath rest, the truth of the world begins to sink in: you are not necessary. That's the beauty of grace.

In sabbath, we realize that even the most important of us can disappear, and the world will go on. But if Christ, the sustainer of the universe, were to disappear, everything would fade away.

Sometimes I think back to Matteo Ricci's memory palace. I picture how even the most brilliant, rich, and successful of us are still utterly dependent on the goodness of Christ to sustain the world, moment to moment to moment.

Christ is generous. All things and the memory of all things live on. He sustains us still in this moment. And in this next one. Sabbath, then, is the essence of our salvation. We can rest because God has done all that needs to be done.

Looking back, I delight in the irony that it took a Chinese doctor to teach this American missionary to sabbath—when I remember the moment he put his hand on my shoulder, looked me in the eye, and told me in his own language that I was allowed to rest.

We are all looking for someone to look us in the eye and tell us we've done enough, that it's okay to stop. This is the good news of the gospel. Jesus tells us this himself: "Let me teach you, because I am humble and gentle at heart, and you will find rest for your souls" (Matthew 11:29).

Many, many people believe that being a Christian means *trying* to be a good person. They think that God likes "good" people and forgives those who try hard enough.

This is not true! Don't believe a word of it. Even worse, it is the most burdensome lie ever told. Here's the truth: we are messed up beyond belief, but loved beyond belief, and that is the one thing worthy of our belief.

If you've lived your life believing that you can earn your worth, that you can earn your salvation by outweighing the bad with the good, that you can justify your place in this world through the college you get admitted to or status you achieve—come and rest!

In Jesus, there is peace that no amount of effort can accomplish. He lived the good life we all try to live. He did it all. He sacrificed everything. He always said the right thing. He always knew what to do and where to go.

And where did it get him? It got him killed. People hated him.

They stripped him naked and hung him on a cross. He lived the life we're all trying to live, and he was answered with death. But it was all for love. It was all for you!

He stayed up all night in the garden of Gethsemane so you could sleep. He finished his work on the cross so you could rest. He let the world break him so it doesn't have to break you. He rose from the tomb so all your aspirations won't end in the grave.

LOVE BEFORE HABITS

> GOD'S LOVE FOR US REALLY CAN CHANGE THE WAY WE LIVE, BUT THE WAY WE LIVE WILL *NEVER* CHANGE GOD'S LOVE FOR US.

If you've read any of this book thinking you can muster the good life out of a few daily and weekly practices, you're reading it backward. Love has first come to us. Anything and everything else we do comes after. All these things are simply a response to this astounding love.

Christians do things, sure. Now that Christ is risen, there are all kinds of beautiful ways to live. All kinds of people can be shown his love. Many languages can be learned.

There is so much good work to do alongside the Redeemer of the world, and so many habits to practice and cultivate. But it comes out of God's love, not our need.

If you place habits before love, you will be full of legalism. But if you place love before habits, you will be full of the gospel. God's love for us really can change the way we live, but the way we live will *never* change God's love for us.

THINK ABOUT IT . . .

1. Taking a sabbath is one of the Ten Commandments. Why does God think resting is that important?

2. Resting looks different depending on whether you're in high school, college, or somewhere else in life. What would sabbath look like in your phase of life? What day would be best for it?

3. Why do so many of us put our worth in our work, instead of resting in God's great love for us? What is spiritually valuable about realizing that we can't finish everything?

WEEKLY HABIT 4

SABBATH REST

THE HABIT AT A GLANCE

The weekly practice of sabbath rest teaches us that God sustains the world—we don't. To embrace our limitations and our love for God, we stop our usual work for one day of rest. Sabbath is a gospel practice because it reminds us that the world doesn't hang on what we can accomplish, but rather on what God has already accomplished for us.

THREE WAYS TO START

Pick a twenty-four-hour period. I find Saturday sundown to Sunday sundown to be the best for my job, my family, and most of my friends' lives. A friend told me that while he was in grad school, his sabbath was from noon on Saturday until noon on Sunday. The important part is picking a period of time and communicating it to the people who need to know or who are joining with you in sabbath.

Doing and not doing. You may need time to figure out what makes a worshipful and restful sabbath for you. If you're just starting, it may help to write down three things to do and three things you want to avoid. They may change as you go, but writing them down will help you to not only think it through but also be accountable.

Communal sabbaths. Keeping sabbath in community is a great way to get into a rhythm. Honor the sabbath in a friend group by having a regular communal meal or coffee time. To keep it restful, meet at a favorite coffee house. You can also trade off going to friends' houses.

THREE CONSIDERATIONS

Work on the weekends. If you need to do homework or work a job for a couple of hours or all day on Saturday to be able to take off Sunday, then do it. My family life is often better when I spend Saturday afternoon at the office so I can take off all of Sunday. This is much different than working a couple of hours both days. It's worth focusing and finishing so you can then focus on rest and realize that, in Jesus, all is finished.

Rest to reinvigorate. Studies show productivity drops off sharply after fifty hours of work per week. Don't waste your time by having projects take longer than they should. You might feel like you have the energy and mental ability to push through with four AP classes, a part-time job, and being president of student council. But taking time off to do something that refills you is an important practice to implement now so you can be a whole person later.

Electronic sabbaths. The most important way you might sabbath is to turn off screens. I usually don't touch my computer during my sabbath day, but sometimes watching a baseball game with my family is the heart of sabbath for me. I recommend doing a month of sabbaths with no screens at all to get a real sense of what it's like. Then if you find that watching Netflix is your essence of sabbath, build it back in. Cutting the cord for a while gives you a taste of a weekly way of life that you may not know existed.

We can rest because God has done all that needs to be done.

CONCLUSION

THE RULE OF FAILURE

When people fall down, don't they get up again? When they discover they're on the wrong road, don't they turn back?
JEREMIAH 8:4

My life is riddled with failure. My friends know it. My family knows it. God knows it.

Years ago, I was leading a group of people through the Common Rule habits. One morning I woke up planning to write an email to check in and ask how everyone's habits were going. Just one problem (actually several): I was failing at my own habits.

1. The previous evening I'd failed in a fast.
2. I'd ignored my morning prayer because my son woke up early and I was upset.

I can never seem to do what I want to do—ever, I thought.

In my anger, I grabbed my phone and started to scroll. My heart was empty and looking for something, anything, to fill it up.

Scripture before phone, came to my mind.

I paused. I'd practiced this habit for so long that it felt weird to start my day on my phone.

This is stupid, I thought. *It's a stupid legalistic rule.*

My mind was aware of the good habit, but my heart didn't want to do it. I tried to justify my bad decision, but I couldn't.

Fine, I'll do it. Ugh.

Instead of randomly scrolling, I opened a Bible reading app. Psalm 27 came up. I began speed reading it; it was an absolute insult to the text.

I was running full speed through this psalm when it felt as if someone laid out a trip wire. I went sprawling face-first onto this line: "One thing I will seek after, to behold the beauty of the Lord" (Psalm 27:4, author's paraphrase).

I stopped. I read it again. Then I read it ten more times.

Suddenly, everything changed. Instead of beating myself up for my failures, I was thinking about how God fills my life with beautiful things.

I was thinking about the way my wife squints her eyes when she turns a page in a book. I was picturing how peacefully my kids sleep. I was seeing the way the sun splashes off the rocks in the James River every evening. I was thinking of good friends, deep conversations, and heartfelt laughter.

I was thinking how everything inside of me was made to behold something beautiful. And, ultimately, how my destiny is to see the face of God looking back at me.

I did write an email that morning. I wrote it one-handed on my phone, on the porch, while holding my son, Coulter. It began with this: "I woke this morning feeling like a failure and a fraud."

No other email has received so many grateful responses. Apparently nothing I ever said about the Common Rule habits was as helpful as talking about failure—because failure is where we live.

That was the morning I realized failure is not the enemy of formation. It is the path to formation with beauty as the destination. How we deal with failure says volumes about who we believe we are and who we really believe God is.

When we trip on failure, do we fall into ourselves? Or do we fall into grace?

My advice: get up, and keep walking toward beauty.

A BEAUTIFUL LIFE

I began this book by describing how these rules, or habits, create a trellis that directs our life. Once we construct this framework, it isn't about *trying* to live right. It's about having our habits take root in God and allowing our lives to grow and bloom.

This is the vision of the apostle Paul in his letter to the Romans. After building his majestic argument for grace alone as the power of God's salvation, he turns to the reader: "Give your bodies to God because of all he has done for you. Let them be a living and holy sacrifice" (Romans 12:1).

Basically, Paul says the natural response to the work of God is to give your whole self to him. Your *whole* life. After all, didn't Jesus present his whole self—his whole life—as a living sacrifice for us?

Then Paul goes on to say, "Don't copy the behavior and customs of this world, but let God transform you into a new person" (Romans 12:2).

If the question is "How does a human being offer a whole life to God?" the answer is *formation*, a word that connotes structure and process. It's about taking a drab brick wall of a life and seeing it transform into something abundantly beautiful.

We celebrate and yearn to live like the people who seem to have been able to concentrate their lives around making the world more beautiful. William Wilberforce in his fight against slavery. Martin Luther King Jr. with his voice for civil rights. Mother Teresa in her service to orphans and the terminally ill. They seemed to focus everything on the important things.

This vision is the goal of a life guided by habit.

Yet what we so often overlook in our hunt for beautiful lives is the striking plainness of the moments that make up the days that make up our lives. What we often overlook in our heroes are the one million tiny (but so carefully chosen) habits that got them there. By overlooking them, we overlook the way the most ordinary habits of limitation create the most extraordinary lives of meaning.

Anyone who studies habit inevitably happens upon the same surprise: how ordinary and simple the building blocks of the most complex and beautiful things are.

THE CONNECTION BETWEEN THE ORDINARY AND THE EXTRAORDINARY IS THROUGH VERY SMALL HABITS.

Leonardo da Vinci began painting tiny brush strokes on a piece of poplar wood in 1503. Fourteen years and hundreds of thousands of brushstrokes later, that piece of poplar was the *Mona Lisa,* a masterpiece that experts are still x-raying to figure out how he painted impossibly thin brush strokes.

Remarkable things are built from the smallest persistent actions or by subjecting ourselves to limitations.

The connection between the ordinary and the extraordinary is through very small habits. Small things build up to great works of art. And limits pave the way for new kinds of beauty.

FAILING BEAUTIFULLY

Have you ever heard of *kintsugi*? In Japan, artists don't throw away a broken bowl. They repair it by inlaying gold or other precious metals. The new bowl is stronger than the old one, and the gold draws your attention to the cracks. The scars are the design; it's what you're supposed to see. The beauty is in the brokenness.

For those who focus inward on themselves—which is the default legalistic gaze—failure destroys them. Instead look outward. Look for beauty, and you'll see that failure is making *you* the work of art. You are more beautiful and stronger because of the fault lines.

My life is like a game of Whac-A-Mole. I use one habit like a hammer to bang down one failure, then a new one pops up. Maybe you can relate.

There is no program that can simplify the fractures of my heart. There's no rule that can contain my chaos.

All of this is true *now*. Right now as I'm writing about formational habits, it turns out I'm a mess.

People often ask what my "life verse" is. Easy pick: "I have discovered this principle of life—that when I want to do what is right, I inevitably do what is wrong" (Romans 7:21).

Here is the point. Look at me or at any other human being long enough, and you'll see nothing but a hypocrite. This will be true of every human being ever, no exceptions but Jesus. But if you stand next to me and look where I'm looking, then we'll both see Jesus. He is the one who lived the beautiful life. He's the life given for us. The gold of his resurrection inlays all our fault lines.

A beautiful life inspires a beautiful life. Even when imitating Christ is a sorry echo of the real thing, it's worth doing, because something worth doing is worth doing badly.

This is the ethic of the search for beauty, which is the only true worship. Like Mary, the sister of Lazarus, pouring perfume on Jesus' feet (see John 12:3), you lose yourself enough to embarrass yourself. You try anything, because you're lost in your desire to honor the one you love.

Those are the kind of habits worth cultivating—little habits of love, not carried out for success, not carried out to prove who we are, but cultivated because of a longing to love God and neighbor.

Those are the kinds of habits that become the tiny strokes in the *Mona Lisa*. They become the days that become a life spent looking at the Beautiful One and making the world more beautiful.

This is a more beautiful life: one worth the constraints, one worth the failures. A life that follows the one named Jesus, who with a glance can catch the heart off guard—and fill it with peace, hope, contentment, and love.

THINK ABOUT IT . . .

1. If you've tried these habits at all, then you've probably already failed. What have your failures taught you about grace, about Jesus, and about yourself?

2. How can being honest about our failures and sharing them with others be helpful? Why do you think people responded so gratefully to my email about my personal failure?

3. Following these habits won't change God's love for us, but God's love for us can and should change our habits. How might this knowledge change your motivation to persevere and build your life on the trellis of these rules?

THE COMMON RULE FOR YOUTH GROUPS

The Common Rule can be practiced alone, but is often best when practiced in community. That's where the "common" part comes from. Talk to your youth pastor about practicing the Common Rule at your church. Your leader can make use of the videos or resources at www.thecommonrule.org and do the following.

1. Create small groups. It's best for people to be divided into groups when trying habits, whether small groups or accountability groups. Make sure these groups are small enough communities that people can talk about their experiences. As group members recognize some of their bad habits, it's very important to be able to process failure and difficulties with others in a safe environment.

2. Cast a vision for practicing the habits. People have to understand the *why*, otherwise these habits won't make sense. It's not just about the things you're going to stop doing, which is simple behavior management. And it's not even about the things you are starting to do. The reason for doing any of this is to lean into these habits or structures (think back to the trellis) that help guide us as we learn and grow. These practices allow God to transform us into who he wants us to be, as we grow in genuine relationship with him and with others.

3. Emphasize the voluntary nature. Encourage everyone to get the book. Then they can read up on one habit and experiment with it. Have your youth pastor suggest they try to follow along and practice some or all of the habits. It helps to have a core group—whether peer leaders, small group leaders, or a group that's simply excited about the idea—lead the charge by committing to try the habits and guide others. Note that formational habits can't and must not be forced. People have to be personally motivated. This often comes when they see or read how others are changed by the habits.

4. Set a time frame. A month works well for getting started. January is a good month to test new habits, or even the first month of the school year. A church season such as Lent or Advent is also a great opportunity to get started. A week is usually too short for a youth group. Whatever you do, make sure everyone knows how long they'll be trying out habits. At the end, talk about the successes, failures, and plans to continue the habits into the future.

NOTES

WHAT IS A HABIT?

1 David Brooks, "The Machiavellian Temptation," *New York Times*, March 1, 2012, www.nytimes.com/2012/03/02/opinion/brooks-the-machiavellian-temptation.html?smid=url-share.

2 Charles Duhigg, *The Power of Habit* (New York: Random House, 2012).

3 Angelica Stabile, "97% of Kids Use Their Phone During School Hours and Beyond, Says Study," *New York Post*, October 1, 2023, https://nypost.com/2023/10/01/97-of-kids-use-their-cell-phone-during-school-hours-and-beyond-says-study/.

4 Claire McCarthy, "Anxiety in Teens Is Rising: What's Going On?," American Academy of Pediatrics, November 20, 2019, www.healthychildren.org/English/health-issues/conditions/emotional-problems/Pages/Anxiety-Disorders.aspx.

THE EIGHT HABITS OF THE COMMON RULE

1 "23 Weird Old American Laws You Won't Believe Were Passed," yahoo!life, April 13, 2023, www.yahoo.com/lifestyle/23-weird-old-american-laws-151602979.html.

DAILY HABIT 2: ONE MEAL WITH OTHERS

1 "Desires, Barriers and Directions for Shared Meals at Home," The Hartman Group, June 2017, www.fmi.org/docs/default-source/familymeals/fmi-power-of-family-meals-whitepaper-for-web.pdf?sfvrsn=13d87f6e_2.

2 "The Benefits of the Family Table," *American College of Pediatricians*, February 2021, https://acpeds.org/position-statements/the-benefits-of-the-family-table.

3 By modern world, I have in mind the way Charles Taylor, and those who have interpreted him such as James K. A. Smith, mean when they use that phrase. See James K. A. Smith, *How (Not) to Be Secular: Reading Charles Taylor* (Grand Rapids, MI: Eerdmans, 2014).

4 Madeleine L'Engle, *Walking on Water: Reflections on Faith and Art* (New York: Random House, 1980), 191.

DAILY HABIT 3: ONE HOUR WITH PHONE OFF

1 Erika Edwards and Kate Snow, "Kids and Teens Are Inundated With Phone Prompts Day and Night," NBC News, September 26, 2023, www.nbcnews.com/health/health-news/teens-inundated-phone-prompts-day-night-research-finds-rcna108044.

2 Trevor Haynes, "Dopamine, Smartphones & You: A Battle for Your Time," Harvard University Blog, May 1, 2018, https://sitn.hms.harvard.edu/flash/2018/dopamine-smartphones-battle-time/.

3 Julia Jacobo, "Teens Spend More Than 7 Hours on Screens for Entertainment a Day," ABC News, October 29, 2019, https://abcnews.go.com/US/teens-spend-hours-screens-entertainment-day-report/story?id=66607555.

4 Elia Abi-Jaoude, Karline Treurnicht Naylor, and Antonio Pignatiello, "Smartphones, Social Media Use and Youth Mental Health," *Canadian Medical Association Journal,* February 10, 2020, www.ncbi.nlm.nih.gov/pmc/articles/PMC7012622/.

5 Allison Aubrey, "How to Help Young People Limit Screen Time—and Feel Better About How They Look," NPR, February 26, 2023, www.npr.org/sections/health-shots/2023/02/26/1159099629/teens-social-media-body-image.

6 See Cal Newport, *Deep Work* (New York: Grand Central Publishing, 2016).

DAILY HABIT 4: SCRIPTURE BEFORE PHONE

1 Jingjing Jiang, "How Teens and Parents Navigate Screen Time and Device Distractions," Pew Research Center, August 22, 2018, www.pewresearch.org/internet/2018/08/22/how-teens-and-parents-navigate-screen-time-and-device-distractions/.

WEEKLY HABIT 1: ONE HOUR OF CONVERSATION WITH A FRIEND

1 C. S. Lewis, *The Four Loves* (New York: HarperCollins, 1960).

2 Sherry Turkle, *Reclaiming Conversation: The Power of Talk in a Digital Age* (New York: Penguin Books, 2015), 36.

3 Turkle, *Reclaiming Conversation,* 23.

4 Daniel De Vise, "Teens Are Spending Less Time Than Ever With Friends," *The Hill Blog,* June 7, 2023, https://thehill.com/blogs/blog-briefing-room/4037619-teens-are-spending-less-time-than-ever-with-friends/.

5 Turkle, *Reclaiming Conversation,* 143.

[6] Kira M. Newman, "How Long Does It Take to Make a Friend?" *Greater Good Magazine,* May 25, 2018, https://greatergood.berkeley.edu/article/item/how_long_does_it_take_to_make_a_friend.

WEEKLY HABIT 2: FOUR HOURS OF PHYSICAL ACTIVITY

[1] "What Are the Surprising Benefits of Youth Sports Programs?" *Scripps Health,* March 16, 2023, www.scripps.org/news_items/7580-what-are-the-surprising-benefits-of-youth-sports-programs.

[2] Tamera Clifton, "Exercise for Teenagers: A Complete Guide," *Healthline,* April 13, 2022, www.healthline.com/health/fitness/exercise-for-teenagers.

WEEKLY HABIT 3: FAST FROM SOMETHING FOR TWENTY-FOUR HOURS

[1] Speech given by Dr. Martin Luther King Jr. at Stanford University on April 14, 1967, www.rev.com/blog/transcripts/the-other-america-speech-transcript-martin-luther-king-jr.

ABOUT THE AUTHOR

Justin Whitmel Earley is a lawyer, author, and speaker from Richmond, Virginia.

He graduated from the University of Virginia with a degree in English literature before spending four years in Shanghai, China, as a missionary. Justin received his law degree from the Georgetown University Law Center and he now owns and runs Earley Business Legal, his business law practice in Richmond, Virginia.

His first book, *The Common Rule: Habits of Purpose for an Age of Distraction*, was published with InterVarsity Press in 2019. He frequently speaks at businesses and legal events on habits, technology, and mental health. Justin also speaks at churches and conferences on habits, spiritual formation, and parenting.

Additionally, he is the author of *Habits of the Household: Practicing the Story of God in Everyday Family Rhythms* (Zondervan, 2021) and *Made for People* (Zondervan, 2023), a book on the spiritual discipline of friendship.

Justin also writes fiction and poetry, and is the author of a forthcoming children's book. He is married to Lauren and together they have four sons: Whit, Asher, Coulter, and Shep.